Dr. Le Cara's Approach to Restriction Training

Move Better. Feel Better. Live Better

By Ed Le Cara, DC, PhD, MBA, ATC, CSCS
Board Certified in Sports Medicine
Board Certified in Rehabilitation

Table of Contents

About the Author
What is Blood Flow Restriction Training (BFRT) ?
History of BFRT
Mechanism of action of BFR
Benefits of BFR training
Risks of BFR training
Contraindications for BFR training
BFR Equipment
The Scientific Evidence Behind BFR
Practical Blood Flow Restriction
Establishing Your Baselines
TRX Suspension Trainer Exercises
VO2 Max – 40% VO2 Max Training Zone
BFR Training Protocols
Quotes

Chapter 1: The Background of Dr. Le Cara's Approach

Ed Le Cara, DC, PhD, MBA, ATC, CSCS
Board Certified in Chiropractic Rehabilitation
Board Certified in Chiropractic Sports Medicine

We can all look back on our lives and see how certain decisions we make will alter our future. I remember being about 10 years old when my Dad said I should go out for the wrestling team. Little did I know my Dad's recommendation would change my life forever. He said wrestling would make me a better football player. I loved playing football. I wanted to be a professional football player when I grew up. If wrestling was going to help my football career, I was all about it. Like most good wrestlers, I lost my first match. I didn't give up, and hard work, great coaches and good genes allowed me some pretty good success on the mat. I also had a pretty good football career, and most of my friends today are people I either wrestled or played football with. So I am grateful to have made sports a big part of my life.

Coming out of high school, I was recruited to some good schools and ended up choosing the University of California at Davis. Davis' wrestling program wasn't great but competed in the Pac10 conference (now Pac12); was only an hour away from my hometown, so my parents could still watch me compete. Even more important was that Davis is one of the top public schools in the nation.

Wrestling at the college level was tough. My biggest surprise was how different the sport was at the Division I level compared to high school. I didn't score a point in the college practice room for almost 4 months. Talk about frustrating! When I did score my first points, I remember lying off to the side with tears rolling down my eyes and my teammates clapping and whooping it up for me. These college wrestlers were big, strong, technically sound, fit, and most of all MEAN! No one wants to give up any points to anyone or show any weakness.

The physicality of college wrestling guaranteed one thing...I was consistently tweaked and injured. My athletic trainer, Lisa Varnum, at UC Davis, was always there to help patch me up and quickly get me back on the mat. I loved being in the athletic training room; talking to other athletes and athletic trainers; getting taped and iced and using the electric stimulation machine; getting recommendations on exercises I needed to do to overcome my tweaks and injuries. I knew during that time, I wanted to devote my life to helping athletes get back to their sport. Over 20 years later, this devotion has morphed into me guiding people back to activities they love as an occupation.

Lots of hard work on the mat, in the weight room, watching film and running (lots of running) started to pay off. I finally started beating some really quality opponents. My junior year I beat the previous year's Division II champion, which got me ranked in the top 25 in the nation. I was motivated to continually improve with a goal to earn a birth to the National Championships by placing in the Pac10 championships. This was going to be a tough task because my weight class had #1, #3, #5, and #9 in the nation at my weight. That was okay with me because to be the best, you have to beat the best.

Then on December 30, 1994, I was wrestling in a tournament at Oregon State University. Holding on to a 3-1 lead in the semi-final match, I stepped out of bounds and heard the whistle blow. I remember feeling myself go from extremely tense to immediate relaxation due to the blown whistle. My opponent didn't hear the whistle and continued trying to take me down. That split second of relaxation was a big mistake. I remember hearing and feeling a loud, "pop, pop, pop." You could hear my scream across the large auditorium. My knee felt like mush, and I collapsed. I writhed on the mat holding my knee. Anytime I see leg injuries on TV, I still get goosebumps thinking back to that moment.

My wrestling coach, Tim Lajcik, ran over and asked if I was okay. I wasn't. I knew too much. I quietly said, "it's not good. I think I'm done," as tears started to build in my eyes. The split second of relaxation resulted in three out of four knee ligaments being torn. I had been wrestling since I was 10. All the matches, practices, camps, training, and long bus rides were done. I felt the finality in my heart. The psychological component of injury far outweighs the physical pain. I always remember that feeling when I am currently guiding someone back from an injury.

After returning back to campus, I saw our orthopedic surgeon and had an MRI performed. My worst nightmare was confirmed. I had torn the ACL, PCL, and LCL of my right knee. Not only was the season over for me, but the orthopedic said he wouldn't clear me for at least 12 months after the surgery. That meant my senior season would be gone as well. Big time depression set in. I was a leader (captain) and spent 6-8 hours a day with my teammates. Now what was I going to do? I had to get back on the mat.

Since it was winter break, I went home after the New Year for a couple of weeks. I was on crutches and wearing a big brace waiting for the swelling to go down so I could have surgery. My childhood neighbor, Dr. Gary Ogden, who was a chiropractor, saw me outside my house one day and asked what happened. I told him, and he offered to help me to rehabilitate by strengthening and try to avoid the surgery. What he said made sense. I could ALWAYS have the surgery, but what if I could get my leg strong enough by working the muscles around the knee joint? No one had offered this option to me. This concept made total sense. Get the leg as strong as possible and see what happens. I had nothing to lose with this plan.

With the help of Dr. Ogden, my athletic trainer Lisa Varnum, strength and conditioning protocols, and my workout partner and roommate, Derek Vandersloot, I was wrestling again (in a brace) within 4 months. Through this self-recovery process, I discovered the key to rehabilitation was not one specific approach but the integration of many approaches. I unfortunately could never get the knee back to a level where I could compete at a high level. The NCAA's wouldn't allow me to wear a big brace, and I just didn't have the capacity for all the twisting required for the sport. But this experience did open my eyes to alternatives to drugs and surgery for rehabilitation of injuries and guided me to my treatment philosophies to this day.

In my opinion, strength trumps everything when it comes to preventing and overcoming injuries. You see, our joints, tissues and whole body has a certain capacity. See Figure 1 of a diagram 1. I like using this diagram to describe my thought process to patients. I have never seen a diagram like this, so if there is one out there and I need to reference someone, please let me know.

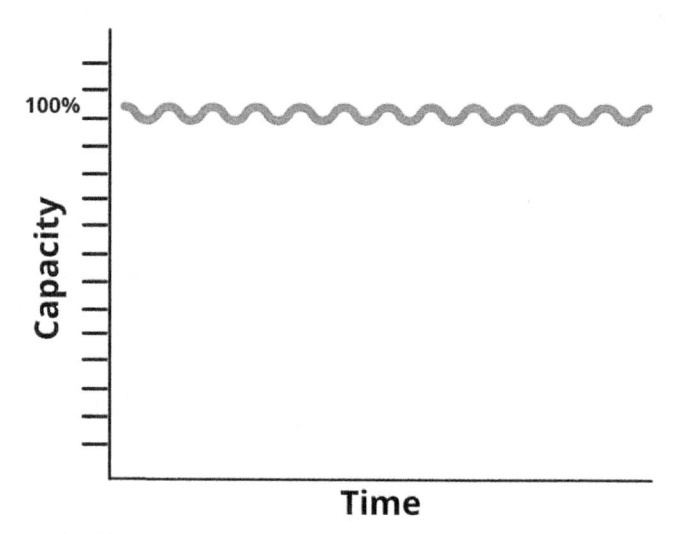

Figure 1. Human Capacity – Everyone has a physical capacity. The capacity goes up and down based on factors like sleep, nutrition, hydration, training, stress.

On the y axis is ones' 100% capacity. Whatever that is. Your capacity is different from everyone else's. You have certain things you physically can do and certain things you can't do. Each of our tissues, joints, muscles all have a breaking point, just like a rubber band. If you stress the rubber band too many times or too far, it will stretch out permanently or eventually break. If you do something that exceeds the capacity of tissue, then injury occurs by stretching or tearing tissue. This can be a specific event like my knee. My body weight, having taken over my knee with my foot planted was too much for the ligaments in the knee to tolerate, so the ligaments tore. The other way capacity is exceeded is through repetitive motions over time. Stress fractures occur in this way. I see a lot of runners in my practice. If they try to run too far and too quick without enough rest in between sessions, stress can occur in the bone and doesn't get a chance to heal and eventually the bone fails (or breaks).

> *"Most repetitive injuries occur from doing too much too quickly after doing too little for too long"*
>
> - Unknown Author

The red dotted line in the figure is demonstrating your capacity over time. Your capacity is not stagnant. A bank account is never the same amount two days in a row. Small changes, like interest, make the bank account grow a little, and large purchases like a car make it go down. Your body capacity works much in the same way. Sleep, diet, hydration, stress, activities, and training all make your capacity go up and down. If I trained heavy deadlifts today, the capacity of my legs to do work tomorrow would be greatly diminished due to delayed onset muscle soreness or DOMS. DOMS is your bodies response to intense exercise: pain, decreased range of motion and decreased torque to prevent you from repeating the previous bout of intensity and forcing you to rest so you can recover.

If I train regular enough (at least 5 days per week) and mix in both aerobic exercise and heavy resistance training, sleep well, eat well, stay hydrated, deal with stress, and stay spiritually strong, our bodies will continue to increase their capacity over time. Meaning you can do more and more even as we get older.

See Figure 2. The purpose of this graph is to show you have your capacity (red dotted line) increasing over time when you exercise at high enough intensities, often enough and over a long enough period. Please note when the capacity begins to increase. Research demonstrates around 12-16 weeks is required for strength and aerobic capacity increases. A little sooner for deconditioned individuals and a little longer if one is already trained and fit.

Unfortunately, most people do not do exercise at a high enough level often enough and stick with it. Instead of even staying at the same capacity level their whole life, they end up losing capacity over time. Most people blame this on the aging process, but in reality, this is a lack of intense activity. See Figure 3.

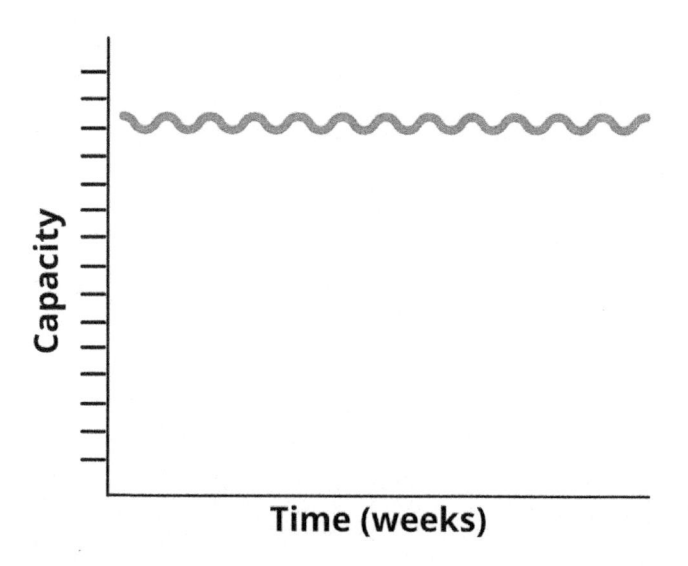

Figure 3 Capacity decreases over time, if we do not stress the body. The loss of aerobic capacity and muscle mass/strength over time becomes significant to the

point that we can't perform daily living activities like walk, shop, travel.

I remember watching my grandfather as he got older. He was really active by traveling and playing golf with his buddies. He really enjoyed his retirement and fruits of his labor. Then one day, he flipped his golf cart while taking a sharp turn a little too fast, and he ended up fracturing his hip. This event was his downfall. After the accident, he spent more time in the big comfy chair watching his stocks go up and his physical capacity (due to inactivity) continue to decline. Finally, he couldn't even go to the store by himself. He got really angry with the world, including his family. His cognitive ability started declining rapidly. Eventually he passed when he just couldn't do anything anymore.

Vacations, accidents, injuries all derail our fitness program. It is important that we keep our sedentary times to a minimum, and we get back to fitness as soon as possible. Otherwise, we will end up like my grandfather...slowly losing capacity over time and never getting the capacity back.

I don't know about you, but I know that I don't want to work 50 years and then not be able to enjoy my retirement. I still have many bucket list items to accomplish like thru hike the Appalachian trail, backpack Europe, and travel the world. Too much on the line to become deconditioned and stuck inside.

In order to improve our capacity, we have to train at a level our brain and body registers as stressful. This is a really important concept for every human being. If we do not stress our body regularly (about every day) at a high enough intensity (at least 65% of our maximum), our capacity goes down over time. Some people think it is age that forces decline of capacity, but this is not true.

Even worse is when someone like me gets injured. We tend to take time off from activity while recovering and trying to overcome pain. This time off leads to atrophy of muscle and aerobic conditioning. We start losing muscle mass as soon as 7 days after the injury and lose aerobic conditioning within 2 weeks. In fact, one can lose up to 30% of muscle mass in just ten days due to disuse like when our arm is in a cast to heal a broken bone.

After the injury and subsequent decrease in function, usually the first couple of weeks is focused on reducing swelling and decreasing pain. Once the pain is gone our capacity is not nearly what it was prior to being injured. We need to expect that our bodies will take a couple of months, at least, to return to pre-injury size and strength. See Figure 4. Unfortunately, we don't think about our injuries this way, and once we get out of pain, we want to return to the activities we were doing prior to getting injured. Since the demand was higher than we can tolerate (why we got hurt in the first place) and now our capacity is even lower than what it was prior to getting injured, we aggravate our injury again. We then take even more time off to 'heal.' Then we try to return to activity again, and we can't tolerate it because the demand is above our capacity, and we reinjure the tissue again. We go back and forth with this until we decide that we just can't do the activity anymore whether it is running or Crossfit or swimming, etc.

Most of my clinical time with patients is figuring out how much capacity their injured tissue currently has and how to load the tissue in a way so people can stay active yet not keep re-injuring the tissue. The other part of my time is spent talking patients off the ledge during their frustration of not being able to do 'what they were able to do when they were younger.'

Since I do classify myself as a manual therapist, where does manual therapy and body work fit into the recovery equation? Well, after doing this for over 20 years, I have discovered manual therapy is only a small portion of the recovery process. I think manual therapy is important to help heal tissue, reduce pain and increase range of motion so people can be active. Most important though is managing this 'Capacity versus Demand scenario I have described. The 60-90 minutes with me a week (in the early phase of injury) is important, but managing the other 6 days and 22 hours per week is where recovery and true rehabilitation occurs.

Since my personal injury, I have been searching for information, techniques or products that help me guide my patients to recover faster and get back to the activities they love. Blood Flow Restriction is the technique I have been searching for. With over 200 peer reviewed journal articles to support BFR usage, the scientific evidence is clear: Blood Flow Restriction training can help (almost) everyone be stronger, bigger and more aerobically sound. This equates in helping individuals do the things they want to do, like travel and participate in activities. I wrote this book to guide individuals to use BFR in a safe and effective way. How does BFR change the way we look at this Capacity Vs. Demand scenario? First, the time to adaptation is much faster. If strength and size usually develop over 12-16 weeks, we can get the same results starting in just 2-4 weeks. This helps us mentally want to continue because we all want results RIGHT NOW. What if your goal was to lose weight, and I put you on a diet, but you didn't lose even one pound for 12 weeks? After a couple of weeks, you would be very frustrated and think the program is not working for you. Just the effort it takes to perform BFR session to session will motivate you to continue because even though you will use light weights, the effort will be high.

Secondly, many people who are injured, de-conditioned, or elderly cannot lift heavy weights thus could never achieve muscle size and strength gains. With BFRT, we can use light weights and still get almost the same size gains as heavy lifting without the muscle damage or injury risk to lifting heavy weights.

Thirdly, using BFR has been shown to decrease pain levels. Most exercises will accomplish pain reduction but not exercise intensity required to increase size and strength. Exercise is the ultimate modality and natural health optimizer.

There are many ways to use BFRT. From rehab to general training, to body building to bone growth. This book is designed with the general, non-medical public in mind. Although I think everyone will get something out of my research and experience. I will tell you how to increase your aerobic capacity, strength, and size without going too deep in the physiology. If you do want a deeper dive into the research, you can take my online course (www.BFRUniversity.com) or take a live course with me which talks extensively about the literature. You can find my live course schedule at www.edlecara.com.

I really hate talking about myself, but I know many people reading this are going to wonder why they should listen to me in regards to BFR Training? Let me give a brief background just to get some 'street cred' prior to moving on with BFR.

Education: I earned a Ph.D. in Athletic Training and had original research published in a peer-reviewed journal on the topic of motor control of the lumbar spine. I am regularly published in trade journals around the topic of corrective exercise and movement assessment.

I am Board Certified in both Sports Medicine and Rehabilitation. I hold a clinical Doctor of Chiropractic Degree. I hold a Master's in Business Administration with an emphasis in Transglobal education. My undergraduate degree is in Exercise Science with an emphasis in Exercise Physiology.

Experience: I have over 20 years of experience successfully treating musculoskeletal injuries for a variety of different types of athletes and patients. I held a hospital appointment at the Veteran's Administration, Northern California Health Care System in their Brain Health and Wellness Program alongside neurologists, physiatrists, physical therapists, and psychologists while providing treatment for my fellow Veteran's.

I have been the Head Athletic Trainer for various Professional, Collegiate, High School, and Youth Organizations including the San Jose Stealth of the National Lacrosse League. I proudly served in the US Army as a Combat Medic. I was the VP of Sports Science and Human Performance at 24Hour Fitness at their corporate headquarters, where they built me a clinic to serve their executives, employees, and families. Many health and fitness companies consult with me to develop education around their products. Those companies are RockTape, Stroops, OptoGait, and TRX training, just to name a few. I currently see patients on a daily basis in a multi-disciplinary clinic I co-own in Dallas, TX called Body Lounge Park Cities (www.bodyloungeparkcities.com).

I am a professor in a master's Level Athletic Training program teaching soft tissue rehabilitation. I also teach numerous courses in a master's level Exercise and Health Program. I teach internationally on multiple topics, but for the last few years, my focus has been Blood Flow Restriction Training for rehabilitation.

Enough about me…Let's get started in my approach to blood flow restriction training!

Please consult your physician before starting any exercise program, including BFR. All of the recommendations in this book are for healthy individuals.

Chapter 2: What is Blood Flow Restriction Training?

Blood Flow Restriction Training is the ultimate 'biohack.' In essence, we are tricking the brain and body into thinking and responding like they are performing high intensity exercise but only using low intensities. This method opens the door for the injured, elderly or deconditioned to the benefits of high intensity exercise which would normally not be possible.

Blood Flow Restriction Training partially restricts arterial (oxygenated) blood flow into the arms or legs while fully restricting venous blood flow back to the heart while at rest or during exercise. Compression of the artery and vein causes inadequate oxygen supply (hypoxia) in the involved limb. (Manini and Clark, 2009; Larkin et al., 2012). Blood Flow Restriction Training is usually abbreviated using the acronym BFRT or BFR.

BFRT is also known as:
- Occlusion training
- Low-intensity occlusion training
- Vascular occlusion moderation training
- Muscle occlusion training
- Hypoxic training
- Blood flow moderation exercise
- KAATSU

Many researchers have defined BFR with slight variations. BFR...

'...occludes venous return and causes arterial blood flow to become turbulent.' (Manini & Clark, 2009)(Manini & Clark, 2009)

'...involves low load resistance exercise combined with moderate reduction of arterial inflow and a blockage of venous outflow of the working muscles.' (Loenneke et al. 2013)(Jeremy P. Loenneke et al., 2013)

'...limits blood delivery to and from contracting muscles.' (Scott et al., 2014)(Scott, Slattery, Sculley, & Dascombe, 2014)

'...reduce the amount of arterial flow into the limb and restrict venous flow out of the limb.' (Dankel et al. 2018)(Dankel et al., 2018)

'...is a training method partially restricting arterial inflow and fully restricting venous outflow in working musculature during exercise.' (Patterson et al., 2019)(Patterson et al., 2019)

My personal (and favorite) definition is

BFRT is the brief and intermittent occlusion of arterial and venous blood flow using a tourniquet while at rest or exercising. Using this technique, one can use significantly less weight or intensity normally expected for physiological adaptation while still achieving gains in muscle size, strength, and functional capacity.

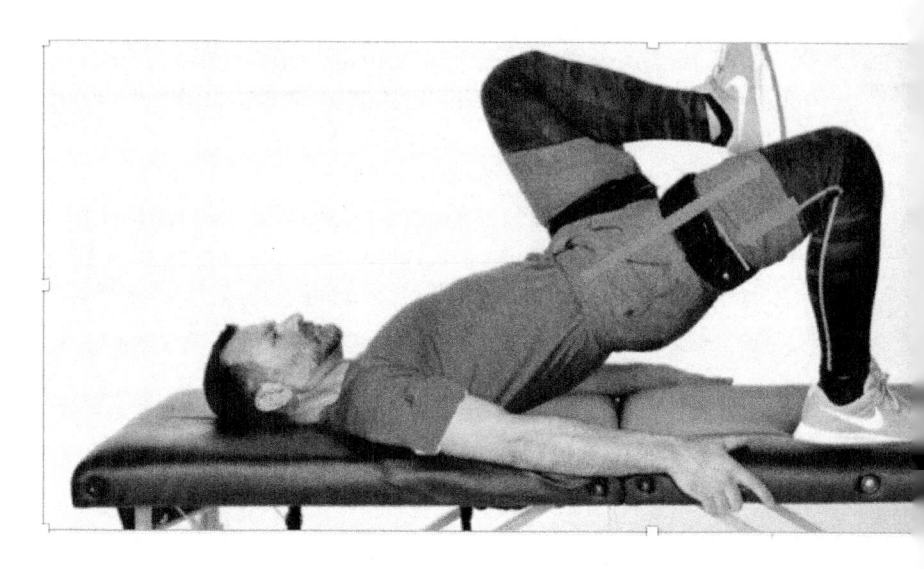

Here you can see me wearing cuffs around both legs while performing a single leg glute bridge exercise. The cuff is restricting the amount of blood into the legs by about 80%. The venous blood returning to the heart has been totally occluded by the cuff which means the venous blood will accumulate in the legs. The limited oxygen rich blood and the fluid buildup in the leg contribute to the benefits seen with BFRT. These benefits will be discussed in future chapters.

The first question I usually get from patients or colleagues is, 'why would I want to restrict blood flow? Isn't blood flow a good thing and lack a blood flow a bad thing?" The answer to that question is usually yes. But in the case of BFRT, by restricting blood flow, you are tricking the brain and body into thinking heavy and intense exercise is being performed. When heavy and intense exercise is performed, the body has to repair any damage that has occurred due to the exercise. If we didn't repair the damaged tissue, we would not be able to defend ourselves, run away from Saber Tooth Tigers, or go hunt and gather for hours on end. Our brains and bodies are still primitive and don't know we have grocery stores down the street for food and most of the time our biggest conflict is wrestling our kids for the remote control. In addition to repair, if the body thinks this new activity is a regular part of our day to day survival, acclimation to the activity will occur over time.

One of the ways we know some damage has occurred to muscle from exercise is through the soreness one experiences after an intense workout. Remember my discussion about DOMS earlier. The body and brain respond by physiologically repairing and responding to the exercise demands. With BFRT, essentially the same repair and adaptation occur after intense exercise but since we use light weights and do not go until failure, little to no muscle damage occurs. With little to no damage, we do not injure tissue further, and no long recovery period is required. In fact some studies have looked at doing multiple BFR training session per day and seeing positive changes in muscle strength and muscle size.

The ability to get physiological adaptation by only using light weight opens the door to many individuals who are limited in the ability to lift heavy weights. For example, in my clinic, patients who are in pain and/or injured come to me. Their injured muscles and joints cannot tolerate heavy weights. Instead of heavy weight, we are forced to use resistance bands, light dumbbells, and body weight exercises. These light weights do not elicit strength; the strength and muscle size increase (hypertrophy) response. If we think about it, why would our body want to increase size and strength unless totally necessary? More muscle mass requires more energy in the form of calories or food. More calories would require more energy expenditure to find and hunt food. This is counterproductive for an efficient existence.

Instead of only using light weights normally required during the rehabilitation period, we can use light weights (the injured tissue can tolerate) and BFRT to accelerate the healing process. The simple addition of cuffs accelerates my patients' return to strength and size in about 1/3 the time. Other individuals who can benefit from BFRT are either those who cannot tolerate heavy weights or cannot risk having muscle damage occur due to high intensity exercise. Those individuals who may benefit the most are:

1. Deconditioned
2. Elderly
3. Injured
4. Healing from Fracture
5. Osteoporotic/Bone Healing
6. Traveling with limited equipment
7. Athletes in the middle of their competitive season
8. Body Builders
9. Those looking for aesthetic improvement (ie. bigger biceps)
10. Pre-Surgical

BFRT is performed by wrapping a device like a cuff, knee wrap or elastic band around the top portion of one's upper or lower limbs. I prefer to use the term cuff and use professional cuffs. The cuff acts as a tourniquet. Oxygenated arterial blood flow from the heart to the limbs is partially reduced. The deoxygenated venous blood, which would normally move from the limbs to the lungs for oxygenation, is unable to go beyond the cuff. Since the veins are closer to the skin (superficial) than arteries, the correct amount of pressure is required to fully block venous return and allow partial arterial flow. We will discuss how to accomplish this pressure in future chapters.

The occluded deoxygenated venous blood pools in the extremities below the cuff. The pooling of blood creates a swelling effect. When I was young and wanting to impress girls, I would do a bunch of push-ups and bicep curls prior to taking my shirt off and heading out to the pool. I would do the exercises to get the muscle pump. The 'pump' made my muscles look bigger than normal. We get this effect x10 when you use BFR. The pump is called cellular swelling and is one of the causes of muscle growth (hypertrophy) when using BFRT.

The other effect of using a cuff on a limb is the decrease in blood flow into the limb. Since arterial blood carries oxygen to the body, if you reduce blood flow, you reduce oxygen into the limb, which we will call a hypoxic environment. The hypoxic environment is another reason BFRT helps to increase size and strength. If you have ever been walking with a friend and able to easily hold a conversation, this is a low intensity exercise. This low intensity exercise is using oxygen as a primary source of energy and can continue for a long time. This situation is analogous to curling a 2.5 pound dumbbell. Eventually you will get tired, but it may take hours before you have to stop due to fatigue. It is more likely you will stop due to boredom before you stop due to the inability to contract the muscle anymore.

If you start running at a fast pace (ie. sprint) in which you can't speak, you will start to feel the burning of high intensity exercise after about 10-20 seconds. The burning feeling is due to the body's inability to utilize an oxygenated environment as an energy source to support the high intensity exercise. Instead of oxygen, your body has to rely on a different energy system that is oxygen poor or termed hypoxic. The running cannot last nearly as long as the walking for many reasons I will discuss in future chapters. This running scenario is also like curling a 25lbs dumbbell. Some people cannot even lift the 25lb dumbbell, and if they can, the time to fatigue and failure is much faster than the 2.5lb dumbbell. Using cuffs, we can create an environment of lifting the 25lb dumbbell but only using a 2.5lb dumbbell. This is an important concept because lifting the 2.5llb dumbbell reduces the amount of stress in the joints and muscles.

If you perform the running scenario long enough and at regular intervals, your body will physiologically adapt, and you will be able to run longer before the burn occurs, and you will be able to go a further distance overall before fatigue sets in. Many people cannot run because of injuries, but most can walk. Many people cannot lift a 25lbs dumbbell, but they can lift a 2.5lb dumbbell. Now imagine creating the hypoxic/burning environment while only walking or lifting the 2.5lb dumbbell because you add BFRT cuffs to the arms or legs. Your body thinks you're running, but you're only walking. Your brain thinks you're lifting 25lbs, but you are only lifting 2.5lbs. You can reduce injury risk and get the benefits of higher intensities and use lighter weights. This is the magic of BFRT.

The second question about BFRT I get is about safety. I will be discussing safety of BFRT in depth. I took an oath at my graduation…"above all else, do no harm." Luckily the topic of safety has been researched, and the resounding answer is BFRT is extremely safe if performed on the right individuals, applied appropriately with quality cuffs, at an individualized limb occlusion pressure. But don't worry, I will discuss the contraindications in detail and make sure you are armed with the information to use BRFT both safely and effectively.

Blood flow restriction (BFR) training has become increasingly popular worldwide. In the United States, BFRT has only been around since 2012, but is gaining popularity. BFRT has been adopted into the military, Veterans Administration, Professional Sports, College Sports, Hospitals, Human Performance Centers, and rehabilitation facilities and clinics across the land. In 2018, the American Physical Therapy Association declared that BFRT was within the scope of practice of physical therapists. More and more individuals are packing their BFRT cuffs while they travel to ensure they can get a good workout in a shorter time no matter what type of equipment is available at the hotel gym. As of this writing, I have taught 1,000's of people in both my live workshops and online course. The word about BFRT is getting out, and I am grateful to have been exposed to BFRT early on and been able to help my patients recover faster and more efficiently.

Chapter 3: History of BFR:

In 1966, at the age of 18, Yoshiaki Sato was attending a Buddhist ceremony in Japan. While sitting in the traditional Japanese posture ("seiza") on the floor for an extended period of time, his legs went numb. He could barely stand the pain any longer with his legs bent underneath him. Out of desperation, he began to massage his calves in an attempt to relieve the discomfort. Sato then realized his blood circulation was blocked in his calves as he was sitting directly on his feet. This was when he conceived the original idea of BFR training. This moment of inspiration led him to envision the original concept of blood flow moderation training and to pursuit a lifetime of exploration, research, and discovery in the field.(Global)

Over the next 7 years, Sato experimented on himself by applying different bicycle tubes, ropes, and bands at different pressures on various parts of his body. He methodically kept track of what type of bands and pressures worked and what experiments did not. With years of detailed trial and error, Sato gradually developed effective protocols to safely modify blood flow to and from his limbs.

By 1973, at the age of 25, Sato developed the details of Kaatsu Training as it is currently practiced. "Kaatsu training" literally means "training with added pressure." About that time on a ski trip, he fractured his ankle and damaged the ligaments around his knee. The injuries were diagnosed, and the doctors told Sato that it would take 6 months to heal.

"Kaatsu training" literally means "training with added pressure."

With a plaster cast on, Sato rehabilitated himself with Kaatsu Bands applied to his upper leg. He repeatedly applied Kaatsu pressure on and off while doing isometric exercises for 30 seconds on and a few seconds off three times per day. As a result, his muscles did not atrophy, and he fully recovered within 6 weeks.

Between 1973 and 1982, Sato conducted Kaatsu training and developed protocols that were effective for people of all ages and with various kinds of disorders.

In 1994, Sato applied for his first patents in Japan, U.S.A., and Europe as he produced the first Kaatsu Training bands. In 1997, Sato introduced the Kaatsu Instructor educational program where his protocols were shared with coaches, trainers, physical therapists, and physicians throughout Japan. Over 3,000 Kaatsu Instructors were certified.

In the 1990s, Sato began joint research with Professor Naokata Ishii of the Department of Life Sciences, Graduate School of Arts and Sciences, at The University of Tokyo. Other researchers in Japan started to explore the benefits of Kaatsu and published various research results. In 2014, Dr. Sato established the Kaatsu Research Foundation.[i]

Around 2014 is when the benefits of BFRT were starting to be discovered in the United States. Physical Therapist, Johnny Owens, MPT was working with limb salvage patients returning from Operation Iraqi and Enduring Freedom. After developing an exoskeleton with the Chief of Trauma, Joe Hsu and a prosthetist, Ryan Blanck, CPO that would act like a prosthetic. The difficulty those men encountered was the exoskeleton they built was so stiff it could cause injury or not perform properly if the limb was too weak. The majority of limb salvage patients had weakness due to the severe trauma they experienced to the arm or leg. Traditional methods to restore strength and hypertrophy were not applicable to most of his patients. While searching for a solution, Mr. Owens discovered BFRT in the literature. After months of literature reviews and intense discussions with his scientist colleagues and surgeons, Mr. Owens was given the green light to attempt BFRT on his patients.(Owens, 2016) The anecdotal results were amazing. He published a retrospective paper on the first cohort of their patients to undergo BFRT in the Special Forces Journal and have since moved on to prospective clinical trials. (Hylden, Burns, Stinner, & Owens, 2015) Mr. Owens developed Owens Recovery Systems and has taught thousands of rehabilitation professionals (and lectured to even more) on how to use BFRT with their patients. Mr. Owens should be credited with being a pioneer of BFRT in the United States with his education and speaking efforts.

In 2014 my friend, Skylar Richards was the Director of Sports Medicine at FC Dallas of Major League Soccer (MLS). Skylar is one of the brightest minds in sports science and human performance. Skylar is like EF Hutton...if he talks, I listen.

The MLS season is the longest in professional American Sports. When FC Dallas had one of the lowest injury rates in professional soccer under Skylar's direction, as measured by player lost time, I pay attention. Skylar and I were collaborating on a different project, and he mentioned BFRT. I had not heard of BFRT, so I did what most nerds do: perform a literature search. I was blown away with how much research had already been done demonstrating safety and efficacy. I immediately started a deep dive into the literature on the why, how, and how not. I went online to find a cuff set that I could start experimenting with my own training. At that time there were not a lot of affordable options. I searched far and wide for a source to show me what to do in a quick and consolidated manner. Nothing existed. I did the best I could with my own training. When I started to see benefits in my strength and size, I started to use BFRT with my patients. I made a lot of mistakes in the beginning. Nothing catastrophic luckily, but using too little pressure, using too much pressure, doing too many exercises, not performing enough exercises. Believe me when I tell you I want you to learn from my mistakes so you can maximize your experience. If you are learning to use BFRT on your clients or patients, feel confident knowing that if you use the techniques and equipment I recommend, your clients will be safe, and training will be effective.

With all the research I had done and experience I gained, I decided to be the source for people to learn about this exciting technology. Now over 800 research articles have been published relating to BFRT with many more coming. BFRT use will continue to expand dramatically over the next few years as awareness heightens, and more products come to market. I want to be the trusted resource for BFRT.

Chapter 4: How to get Started with BFR

Since I am writing this book for non-medical professionals, I figured I would jump straight to the chase. Here we are going to talk about how to get started using BFRT. There are four (4) steps to get started with BFRT.

Step #1: Safety

If you are healthy, not taking any medications, with no co-morbidities, and have clearance to exercise at high intensities from your health care professional, skip to number 2.

If you are unsure if you should continue, please read the chapter on contraindications and receive clearance from your health care professional. If you need help to make sure you are safe to proceed, but your doctor does not know a lot about BFRT, you can look on my website (www.edlecara.com) for a certified provider near you. You can also schedule a virtual consultation with me to get started.

Step #2: Goals

If it is safe to continue, ask yourself what do you want to happen with BFRT? This step is crucial because this will help determine the frequency and programming of exercise. The first question, is what is start location? Without first setting our current location, it's impossible to figure out how to get where we want to go.

Ask yourself, do you want to...

1. Maintain muscle mass and strength everywhere on my body?
2. Increase muscle mass and strength everywhere on my body?
3. Increase muscle size of a certain muscle group (ie, calves)?
4. Improve your aerobic capacity?

Answering the above questions is important because knowing what you want will help determine the number of days you train per week, for how long, and for what duration.

Step #3: Purchase BFR Cuffs

I go into a deeper dive of why I recommend certain cuffs in chapter 5. If you just want to get started right away, go to www.bfruniversity.com and select the 'products' tab on top. There you can purchase cuffs at a discount.

Step #4: Get Started

For a sample, workout go to www.bfruniversity.com and select 'Programming' tab on top. Go to 'Sample Workouts.'

Chapter 5: Risks of BFR training

Everything we do comes with a risk associated with it. Crossing the street, getting in an airplane, driving a car are all associated with risk. BFRT is no different. Everyone should be assessed for risks and contraindications prior to BFR cuff use. If you have pain exceeding 4/10 (0 being no pain and 10 being unbearable), excessive swelling, any of the contraindications listed below, or are looking to rehabilitate an injury, please get medical clearance from your healthcare provider. You can also go on my website (www.edlecara.com) and find a certified provider near you to help. If none of those options work, you can schedule an online consultation with me.

The research indicates BFRT is a safe modality when an appropriate cuff is used, personalized limb occlusion pressure is used and cuffs are not inflated for longer than 20 minutes at a time. The primary concern from medical providers would be the possible formation of deep vein thrombus (DVT) due to the compression on the vasculature. The numerous research studies performed have indicated performing BFRT is no riskier than normal high intensity exercise. KAATSU training has been applied to over 10,000 people in Japan with an array of different physical conditions. Impairments such as orthopedic, cardiac, respiratory and neuromuscular disease have all been treated. As of publication, no serious side effects have been reported in this population with respect to venous thrombosis. (Nakajima T, Kurano M, Iida H, Takano H, Oonuma H, Morita T, et al. Use and safety of KAATSU training: results of a national survey. Int J KAATSU Training Res 2006;2:5–13).

Normal High-intensity resistance exercise has been shown to increase systolic blood pressure in well-trained young men. (MacDougall JD, Tuxen D, Sale DG, Moroz JR, Sutton JR. Arterial blood pressure response to heavy resistance exercise. J Appl Physiol (1985);58: 785–790.) Even exercise at an intensity of 60% 1RM often causes increased systolic blood pressure (up to 180 mmHg) in older adults. (Ajisaka R. Cardiovascular safety of exercise in the elderly. Jpn J Phys Fitness Sports Med(2003);52(Suppl): 55–64.) Although BFR will reduce blood pressure 30 and 60 minutes after training, it also can raise pressure just as high as conventional resistance training (Domingos E, Polito MD. Blood pressure response between resistance exercise with and without blood flow restriction: A systematic review and meta-analysis. Life Sci. 2018 Sep 15;209:122-131.) Caution is advised in those that are at high risk of stroke but no more so than conventional exercise. If one has been cleared for high intensity exercise, they are cleared for BFR exercise.

The Following Risks Categories Have been Identified in the Research:

- ◊ Patients with poor circulatory systems: Indicators may be varicose veins, limb hair loss, brittle nails, etc.
- ◊ Individuals who have:
    - Arterial calcification
    - Abnormal clotting times
    - Diabetes
    - Sickle cell trait
    - Tumor
    - General Infection

- Hypertension
- Cardiopulmonary conditions
- Renal Compromise
- Clinically significant acid-base imbalance
- Atherosclerotic vessels

◊ Patients who are taking
- Anti-hypertensive
- Creatine supplements
- Beta Alanine Supplements(J. P. Loenneke, Wilson, & Wilson, 2010)
- Hormone Replacement Therapy

The Following Contraindications Have Been Identified and <u>REQUIRE</u> clearance from your medical provider prior to using BFR Cuffs.

◊ Pregnancy
◊ Excessive Swelling (More than 2" circumferential measurement compared to other limb)
◊ Recent (Less than 2 weeks) Surgery
◊ 15 years of age or younger
◊ Venous thromboembolism
◊ Impaired circulation or peripheral vascular compromise
◊ Previous revascularization of the extremity
◊ Extremities with dialysis access
◊ Acidosis
◊ Sickle cell anemia
◊ Extremity infection
◊ Tumor distal to the tourniquet
◊ Medications and supplements known to increase clotting risk
◊ Open fracture
◊ Increased intracranial pressure

- Open soft tissue injuries
- Post-traumatic lengthy hand reconstructions
- Severe crushing injuries
- Severe hypertension
- Skin grafts in which all bleeding points must be readily distinguished
- Secondary or delayed procedures after immobilization
- Vascular grafting
- Lymphectomies
- Cancer

A list of potential conditions and the resultant risks for DVT potential is listed below. As with
exercise in general, a Physician should clear patients with these presenting conditions
before initiating BFR.

- Recent Surgery
- Trauma
- Venous Catheters
- Prolonged Bed Rest
- Plaster Cast
- Long Haul Travel
- Malignancies
- Chemotherapy
- Pregnancy
- Puerperium
- Oral Contraceptives

- ◊ Hormone Replacement Therapy
- ◊ Obesity
- ◊ Infection
- ◊ Inflammatory Disease
- ◊ Smoking
- ◊ Lupus Anticoagulant
- ◊ Genetic Factors for DVT

Those who have been diagnosed with COVID19 should wait 4 weeks to use BFR after a negative PCR test due to the increased risk for hypercoagulation.

Limb Protection

Using cuffs 5cm or wider can help minimize tourniquet risk. To further reduce the risk of cuff shifting and the subsequent burning of the skin, I recommend the use of a tension sleeve directly under the cuff. Go to www.BFRUniversity.com under products to order a special tension sleeve to use under the cuffs. The highest risk will be those with significant adipose tissue or loose skin in the upper arm or upper leg. To minimize the risk of tissue damage under the cuff, avoid placing the cuff directly over wrinkled clothing. Placing the cuff over tight pants like yoga pants or tight shirts has worked fine in my clinic. Instead of placing the cuffs directly on the skin, consider using a two-layer tubular elastic material. Using a two-layer material was shown to be more effective than any other material for reducing skin irritation.(Olivecrona, Charlotta, et al. "Lower tourniquet cuff pressure reduces postoperative wound complications after total knee arthroplasty." The Journal of Bone & Joint Surgery 94.24 (2012): 2216-2221.)

Chapter 6: BFR EQUIPMENT

Just like starting any fitness routine, there will be some equipment necessary to perform BFR. Here is where things can get a bit confusing. What are the differences in the cuffs? Which company should I buy my cuffs from? How much money do I have to spend? Can I get away with a cheaper version and get good results? These are all very good questions. I am going to discuss the different options you will need to consider when purchasing the cuffs and then at the end I will provide a chart of the different options and which companies include those options.

BFR EQUIPMENT ORIGINS

When we think about reducing blood flow to a limb, a surgical tourniquet comes to mind. I mean, the surgeon wants to reduce as much blood to the limb as possible while the surgery is occurring. In addition, surgeries can last many hours so the pressure used or the type of cuff used needs to be efficient and as safe as possible. What the cuffs are made of, how wide they are and where they are placed all make a difference.

The most recent tourniquet systems used in surgery are considered 3rd generation tourniquet systems. These 3rd generation tourniquet systems include features individualized for the patient. These 3rd generation tourniquets have cool features like automatically measuring the minimum pressure required for limb occlusion. These features improve the safety and efficacy of the tourniquet in the operating room.

The best BFR systems have used 3rd generation surgical tourniquets as a guide to develop safe and effective cuffs to be used during exercise. Of course, there should be some differences between a surgical tourniquet and BFR cuffs used during exercise. For example, during surgery, the patient is usually asleep and not moving. During exercise the limbs are moving and active, contracting and relaxing both in weight bearing (standing/sitting) and non-weight bearing (lying down) positions which all affect the pressures being used.

EARLY BFR

Belts, knee wraps and elastic tubing have been used to occlude blood flow to the limb during exercise. Considering complications such as nerve and artery injury, skin injury, and pain are consequences of using too high of pressure, high pressure gradients under the cuff and long duration of use, one would want to use the least amount of pressure necessary to occlude the blood flow enough to the get the results one is looking for. Using belts, knee wraps and elastic tubing is impossible to be consistent with the pressures being used or measure the pressures at all. The following factors are taken into place when making safe and effective cuffs:
1. Pneumatic (inflatable) or Practical
2. Cuff Material – Elastic or More Rigid Cuff
3. Cuff Width – Narrow (<5cm) vs. Wide (>5cm)
4. Bladder System – Single Chamber vs Multichamber Air Bladder
5. Internal or External Doppler
6. Automatic Inflation vs Hand Pump
7. Autoregulate vs Standard Regulation

8. Price difference

I will discuss each of these items individually.

Pneumatic or Practical BFR Cuffs

Practical BFR Cuffs are straps or bands that do not inflate. Knee wraps, voodoo floss bands, clinchable belt like straps, and many other materials of different widths, lengths and materials have been used.

Pneumatic BFR cuffs are inflated with a pump. The pump either stays connected to the cuffs with a hose or the hose can be disconnected.

There are pro's and con's to all the cuffs available. I will go into great detail on the only types of cuffs I will use on myself and my patients and why.

Cuff Material

The material can be very stiff or can be very elastic. The ideal material is somewhere in between that is able to be cleaned. Especially if being used by multiple individuals.

Cuff Bladder

Some cuffs are made with bladders (the part of the cuff you fill with air) that are segmented. When the bladder is segmented it is nearly impossible to determine your limb occlusion pressure because full arterial occlusion cannot be determined. This means the pressures you are using are considered arbitrary because we are using our best guess and not determining individualized limb occlusion pressure. The exercises with these bladders can still be difficult but this is not true BFR because you are not occluding venous blood flow and restricting arterial flow. You can tell bladders that are segmented by going over to YouTube or Instagram and seeing people use heavy weights or plyometrics or cuffs on all 4 limbs. If the bladder is continuous, the exercises are much harder. If you try to exercise with all 4 limbs with cuffs on you will reduce stroke volume to the point you may pass out. Harder is not necessarily better but the point is to use equipment that allows one to get the benefits of heavy load training while using light loads. In my opinion, segmented bladders do not accomplish this. SmartCuffs first generation of cuffs used segmented bladders and they quickly switched to Gen2 which had continuous bladders because limb occlusion pressures could not be determined.

Cuff Width

Cuffs are either considered wide or narrow. Wide cuffs are 5cm or larger in width and narrow cuffs are smaller than 5cm. There is a happy medium between cuff comfort and safety as the more narrow the cuff the more pressure needed to occlude the veins. Wider cuffs (to a point) are more comfortable as well.

Pressures Required

Surprisingly, if you look at the published research regarding BFR there are not any consistencies between the cuffs being used for vascular occlusion. The researchers have tried to make consistencies so that we can compare the studies and really pinpoint what is an effective methodology. For example, the study design may be really flawed if one study uses 5cm wide cuffs at 200mmHg of pressure and another study uses 10cm wide cuffs at 200mmHg of pressure. These pressures need to be consistent, so we are comparing apples vs apples to hone in on best practices. One way we have established consistency is using arterial occlusion pressures or aop. We establish AOP with an auditory doppler ultrasound unit or doppler for short. A doppler can be a stand-alone piece of equipment or built into the pump.

Internal or External Doppler:
1. Internal or External Doppler
2. Automatic Inflation vs Hand Pump
3. Autoregulate vs Standard Regulation
    a. Price difference

Originating with just elastic bands and tubing, BFR equipment has morphed into class 1 medical devices. It started out basic and progressed to a more finely tuned process. Just like any other system that was pioneered to improve the scientific process of improving strength and human performance, BFR has come a long way.

BFR tourniquets now range from guessing the correct pressure to manually inflating, and finally to an external doppler that finds the pressure that is necessary. While utilizing bands and tubing is still a choice for some wishing to save money, the technique has evolved to precise tools specifically designed to give you the best results.

BFR Equipment 1. *Tubing used for early blood flow restriction.*

Automated systems are now the gold standard of BFR training. There is some hesitation for someone looking to start utilizing BFR training in regard to automated systems due to the pricing. As a new chiropractor I wanted to experiment with IASTYM tools, so I bought some cheaper tools. They did the job, but weren't the best tools to use on myself or my patients. Once I became sold on the idea that IASTYM was beneficial and could get better results, I started researching and bought the tools with the best design that could give the best results for my clients. These tools handled better, lasted longer, and had a reputation for being the best.

BFR is no different. Tubing and bands can still work for limb occlusion, but it is no longer the best method of training. You can get results. You will not get the best results. The only reason I see for anyone not to use the tourniquet systems is to start BFR training on a budget. However, the problem with that method is the same as any healthcare or wellness situation. How much are you really saving when you consider the cost of not training correctly? Tourniquets, especially automated tourniquets, allow you to find the precise limb occlusion pressure to get you the best results in the quickest amount of time. As a healthcare provider who works with clients in rehab and performance settings, I want to get them back to their prior levels quickly and efficiently. Automated tourniquets give me the greatest advantage at doing just that, and they can give you that advantage too.

For this reason, it is difficult for me to recommend someone use the bands and tubing or cheaper BFR equipment. In my own training I know that when I was using the cheaper equipment that I wasn't using enough pressure because I was afraid I would injure myself. Not having confidence in my equipment cost me better training and wasted time. If you do not have confidence in your equipment it will do the same to you. That is why I always recommend getting a good set of BFR cuffs. That is why I recommend SmartCuffs and stand behind them 100%.

Having the right equipment is paramount to training efficiently and effectively. It's like leaving out an ingredient in your mom's famous cookie recipe. You may still get cookies, but no one wants to eat them. Getting the best results with BFR training requires that you know the correct pressures, cuff width and length, and training protocols. SmartCuffs allows you to dial in your training so you aren't wasting time guessing if you are training correctly. This gives you the safest and most effective workout.

CUFF SIZE

Cuffs come in different sizes to ensure that the correct pressure can be obtained for optimal training. Usually there are 2 different sizes to accommodate the difference between the arms and the legs. Having different cuff sizes is important to get the correct pressure for limb occlusion. If the cuff is too large you will need to use more pressure to get arterial occlusion. If the cuff is too small then you can't get true occlusion and your training will not be the best. There has to be a balance in choosing the correct cuff size. SmartCuffs started with 5 cuff sizes, but through research and training they have settled on 3 different cuff sizes to make sure you are able to meet your needs.

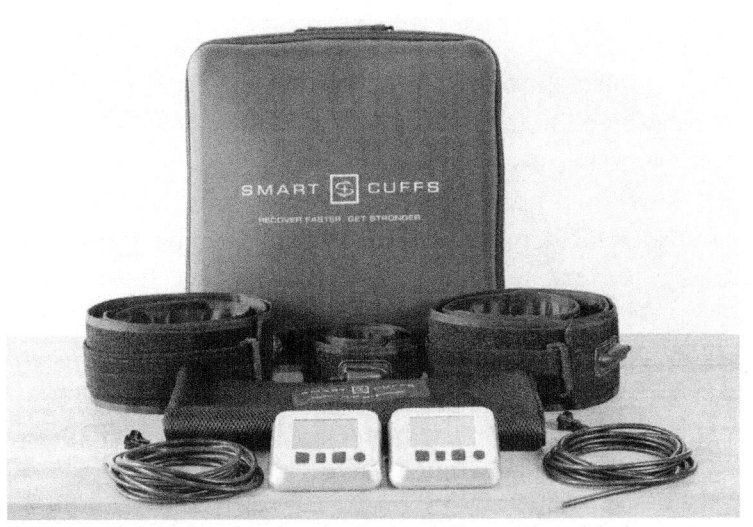

BFR Equipment 2. SmartCuffs Pro Elite. The third generation of SmartCuffs.

When picking the correct size cuff for an individual, it is important to pick a set that correlates with the size of your arms and legs. Measure your arms and legs and then pick the cuff that is able to accommodate your specific measurements.

LIFE EXPECTANCY OF BFR CUFFS

SmartCuffs have a 1-year warranty which is the industry standard right now. They should give you 4 to 5 years of training if you are using them for personal use. Clinically, they should give you approximately 2-3 years of BFR training with your clients.

BFR DECREASES GYM BUDGET

BFR training not only allows you to train harder with less weight. It also allows you to train with less equipment. In my clinic, I no longer have the need for heavy weights to get maximum growth and strength for my clients. The cuffs allow me to pump up the pressure (pun intended) and give clients a great workout without breaking the budget.

You do not need to lift heavy to see the results of doing so. Your body just needs to think you are lifting heavy weights. BFR gives you the benefits of training at a high intensity while using light weights. BFR is especially beneficial for someone who does not have the space for a lot of equipment. It is also perfect if you want to train heavy, but are training alone. There is no need to load the bar to get a great workout when you are using BFR.

Besides the doppler, pump, cuffs, and sleeves (optional), I would purchase some light weights. Ankle weights are great (2.5lb/5lb) and light dumbells (2.5lbs, 5lbs, 10lbs, 15lbs, 20lbs, 25lbs). You can also use a TRX Suspension Trainer and resistance bands if you don't have room for the dumbells.

For a complete list of equipment I recommend, go to www.bfruniveristy.com/bfrequipment

BFR Equipment 2. *BFR training can turn a modified pushup on the wall or bench into a high intensity workout.*

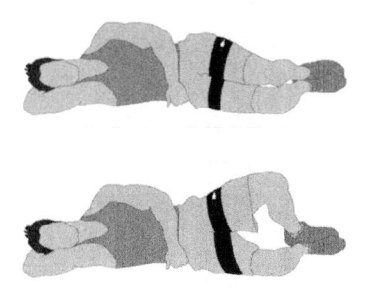

BFR Equipment 3. *BFR training turns this simple clamshell exercise for your hips into a strength training exercise.*

Blood flow restriction training is a great way to train. You can see that the equipment needs are not many and are affordable when removing the need for many different weights and machines that would be needed to get them same results. I recommend SmartCuffs because I believe in them, have tested them for years, and believe them to be the best training option. Whatever cuffs you decide to go with make sure that you feel comfortable using them, know how to optimally get the best results with them, and train with them safely and effectively.

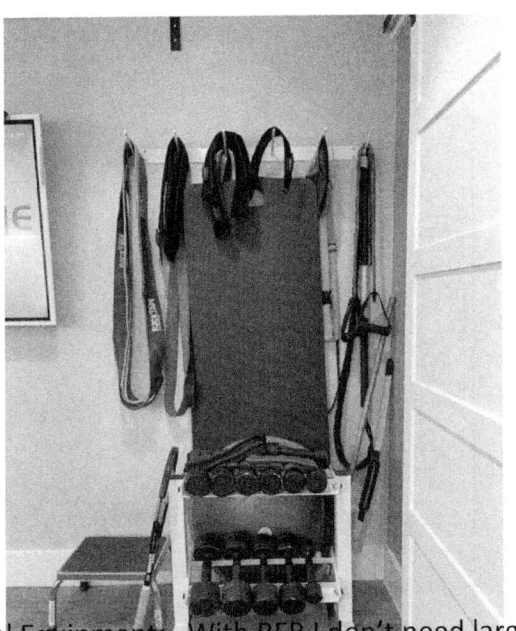

Clinical Equipment— With BFR I don't need larger than 20lb dumbells to rehab my patients with

Insert BFR Equipment checklist:
- Properly fitting cuffs: 1 set for the upper extremity and 1 set for lower extremity
- Pump: (Manual or automatic) – a way to inflate the cuffs
- Doppler Ultrasound: Manual or built into the pump – allows us to know your personalized pressure
- Extremity Sleeves (optional): Protects the skin from shearing of the cuffs

SmartCuff System with 4 cuffs and automated pump/doppler

Cuffs:
Appropriate Sizes for Upper and Lower Extremity

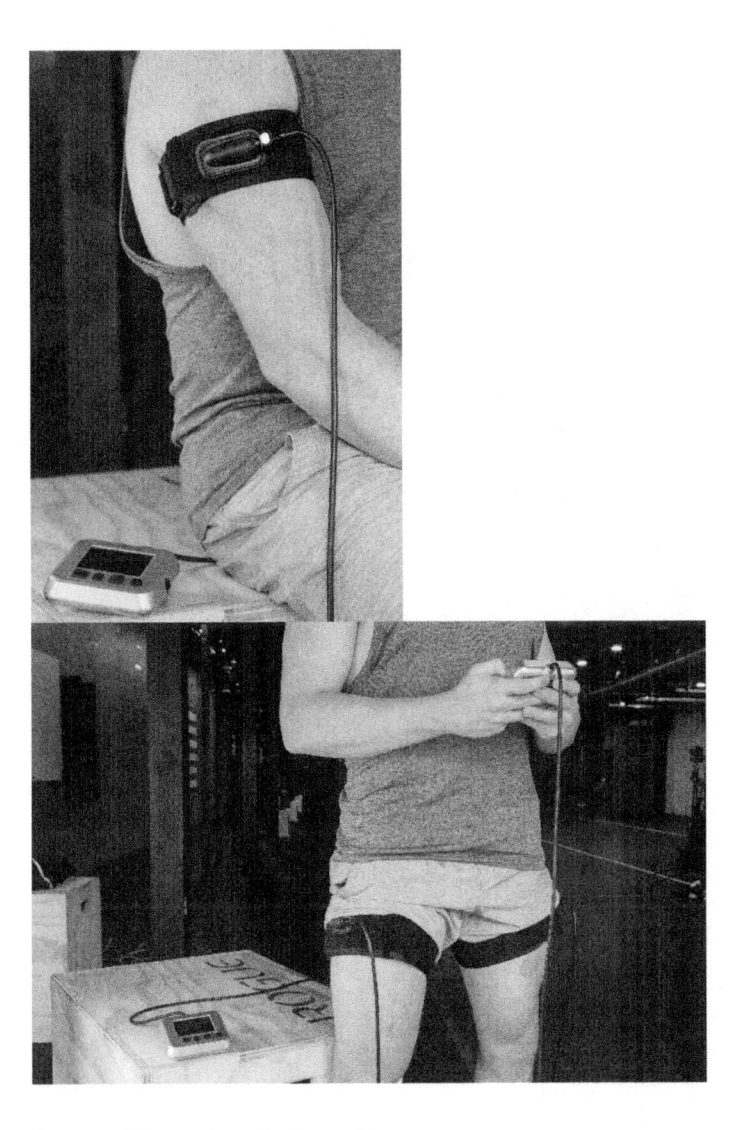

Pump: Manual or Automatic

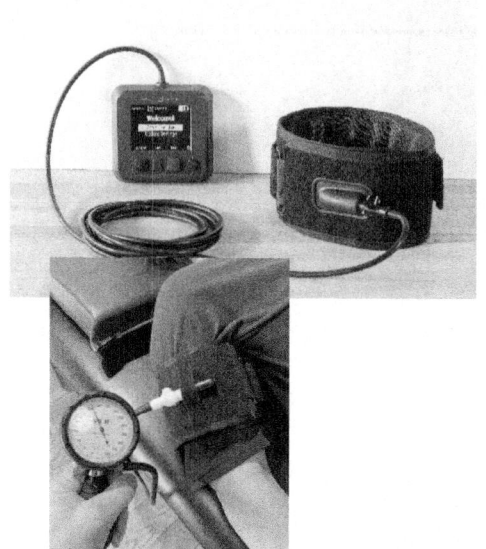

Automatic Pump with built in doppler   Using a manual pump

Dopper: External or Internal

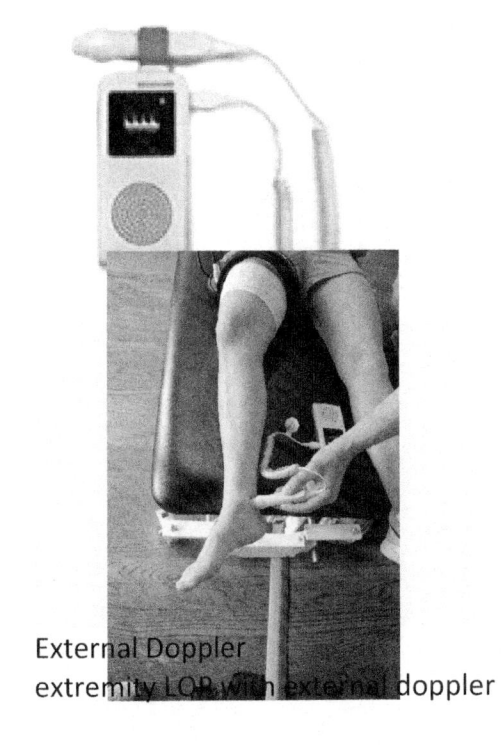

External Doppler　　　　　　　　　　Finding lower extremity LOP with external doppler

Compression Sleeve (optional)

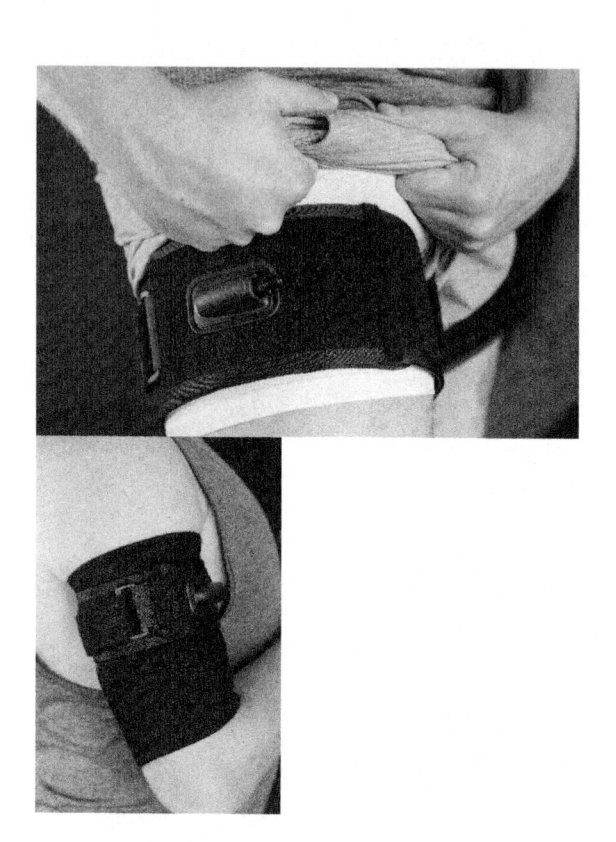

Lower Extremity Cuff over compression shorts
Upper Extremity Cuff on Sleeve

Chapter 7: Establishing Baseline for BFR Training

With any training program you need to establish your baseline first. You know what they say, "You can only change what you can measure"

BFR is no different. In this chapter we will discuss how to establish your baseline using 5 different lifts. These are not the only lifts that you could use to establish your baseline, but will work for the purposes of this book.

In this chapter I will show you how to establish your baselines with cuff size, optimal heart rate reserve, the correct limb occlusion pressures and estimated 1 rep max lifts. The point of this chapter is to take someone who may have never trained with BFR and give them the tools they need to implement BFR training immediately. After reading this chapter you should know what limb occlusion pressures to use, proper cuff sizes, how to establish baselines with 5 exercises, and what weights you will need to get the most out of your training.

Cuff Selection

BFR training can be dangerous or non-effective if you use the wrong cuff. To get the most out of your training and to train in the safest manner you will need to use an FDA listed cuff during your training. to date there are only 2 companies who offer such cuffs, Delfi Medical and SmartCuffs.

As with anything a one-size-fits-all approach is not always the answer, and is certainly not the answer when it comes to BFR training. It is important to have a cuff that is large enough for the limb being occluded to get the best training. This means you may be using a different size cuff for the arms and different size cuffs for your legs.

Measuring The Limb

In this video, I'm going to show you how to measure the limb in order to determine what size cuff to use. So as a guide on the BFR worksheet, if you print that out, it'll show you. What size correlates to the cuff size. But even if we don't have a tape measure, I'll show you how to easily know what size cuff to use.

First thing to do is look for a couple of bony landmarks. The first landmark is the deltoid tubercle of the humerus. Place your thumb and index finger on the front and back aspect of the shoulder joint and run them downwards together. You should make a "V" on your shoulder and come to a point. This is where the deltoid tubercle is and that is your first landmark.

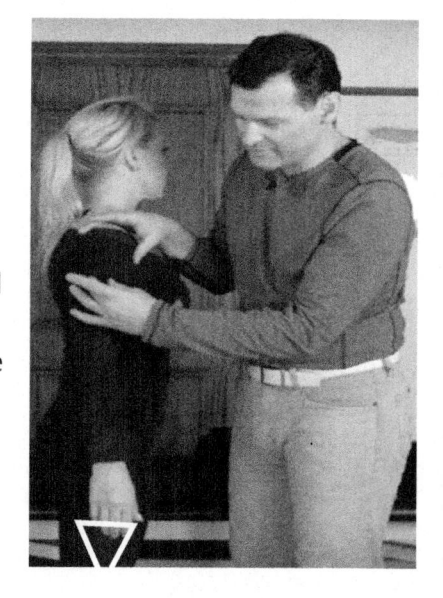

The second bony landmark for the lower extremity is the greater trochanter on the femur. Find the greater trochanter by placing your fingers on the outside of the hip, point your toes, and twist your leg in and out. The bone that you feel under your fingers rotating is the greater trochanter. If you are not absolutely sure of the landmarks; measure at the highest point of the arm (under the armpit) and as high up on the leg as possible.

Next, measure the limbs for proper cuff fitting. Take a tape measure and wrap it around the limb directly below the bony landmark. Make sure the muscles are relaxed and you get a loose measurement. Once you have your measurements you will look at your chosen cuffs to see where the measurement lies in the fitting of that cuff. As a rule, use the smallest cuff that still fully encircles the limb.

If you are using the Smart Cuffs you can printout the BFR worksheet that is listed in the references at the end of (this book/chapter) to keep better track of your cuff size

Calculating Optimal Heart Rate Reserve

You must first calculate your maximum heart before finding your heart rate reserve. We can do this very easily. An estimate of a person's maximum age-related heart rate can be obtained by subtracting the person's age from 220.

$$\text{Maximum Heart Rate (HR)} = 220 - (\text{your age})$$

For example, for a 50-year-old person, the estimated maximum age-related heart rate would be calculated as 220 - 50 years = 170 beats per minute (BPM).

Next, you will find your resting heart rate. The best way to find your resting heart rate is to measure it before you have risen from bedrest. Find the radial pulse. Count the amount of beats in 60 seconds. The first beat is "0".

$$\text{Resting Heart Rate} = \text{BPM at bedrest}$$

Heart rate reserve (HRR) is the difference between maximum heart rate and resting heart rate.

Max HR – Resting HR = Heart Rate Reserve (HRR)

The final number to attain is the training heart rate.

Training Heart Rate = (HRR x Training Intensity %) + Resting HR

For example, take a 19-year-old male with a Resting HR of 70 BPM. Target intensity: 30% HRR for a person with Max HR of 201 BPM and resting HR of 70 BPM has heart rate reserve (HRR) of
131 BPM. To achieve target exercise intensity of 30%:

Training HR = 131 x 0.30 + 70
Training HR = 109 BPM

Finding Optimal Limb Occlusion Pressures (LOP)

There are a couple of ways to find the pressures necessary to occlude blood flow. It can be estimated based on the size of the limb, or you can establish limb occlusion pressure with a doppler. If you don't have a doppler, you can use a distal pulse. If you can't find the pulse I have included a rough chart to give you some starting pressures.

Limb Size

If the circumference of your limb is up to 16 inches your pressure should be between 120 - 160 mmHg. If the circumference of your limb is 16 - 22 inches your pressure should be between 150 - 180 mmHg. Any limbs over the circumference of 22 inches or greater inches should keep the pressure between 180 - 300 mmHg

These are extremely rough estimates. There are too many variables depending on what cuffs you are using, what body position you are exercising in, and many others. I would start with light pressure and use a perceived exertion if I am not measuring LOP. Meaning, to a 7-8/10 intensity (not pain) and do not go above. If the intensity is not at 7-8 then the pressure probably is not high enough or the load is not high enough. Using LOP takes a lot of the guess work out of pressure.

We can use either an external doppler or automatic doppler to establish the safe and effective pressures to use.

Manual Doppler Readings

Once the cuff is placed appropriately on the upper extremity, I will use my doppler ultrasound to find the radial pulse. I have the client relax the limb completely. I then use a small amount of ultrasound gel on the head of the doppler and locate the radial pulse. Next, we inflate the cuff until we can no longer hear the pulse. When the pulse sound disappears, we know that is the amount of pressure needed to occlude the arterial blood flow into the limb. This will be the limb occlusion pressure that you will use in calculating your percentages to perform your workout.

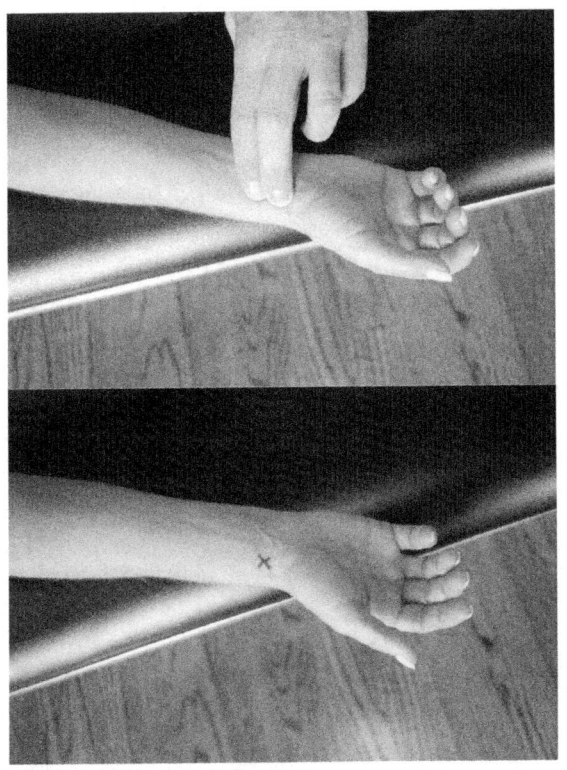

Radial Pulse Location
  Marking the Radial Pulse

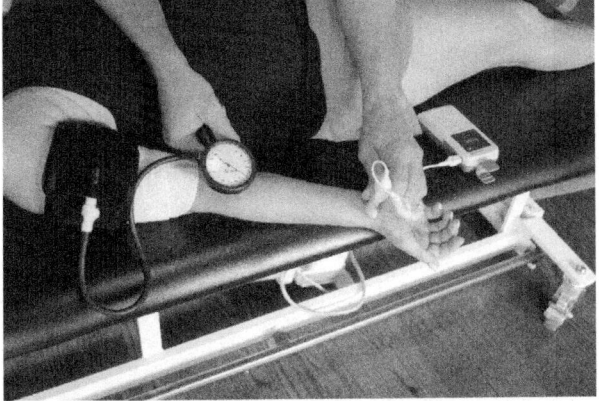

Establishing the upper extremity LOP in supine

I recommend getting your LOP in all three positions: standing, sitting and lying down face up (supine).

We follow the same steps for finding LOP on the lower extremity. In a lying position, make sure palpate the tibialis posterior pulse. This pulse can be found directly behind the medial malleolus of the ankle. Use the doppler ultrasound to find the tibialis posterior pulse along the medial malleoli or inside of the leg. Start inflating the cuffs until the pulse slows and diminishes. Slowly continue until the pulse disappears. Once the pulse disappears, you have the lower extremity LOP for that limb.

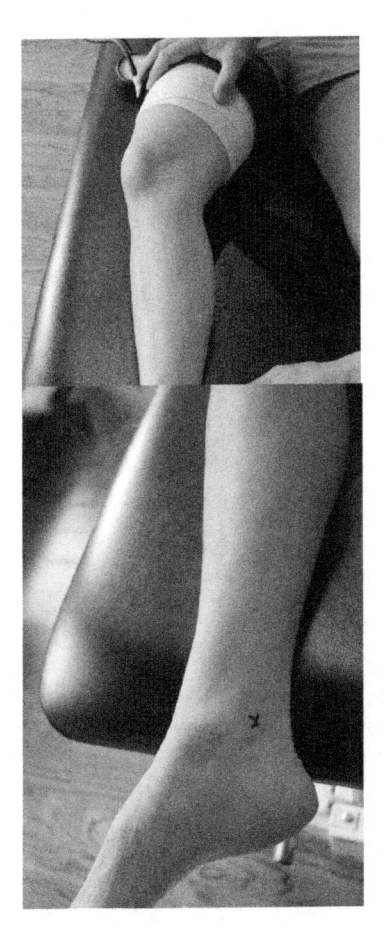

Establishing LOP for the lower extremity on the right leg in standing

This is how you will find the baseline LOP for upper and lower extremities. The training pressure will be anywhere from 30 to 80% of the LOP. I recommend taking baseline LOP measurements on both limbs in all three positions (standing, lying and sitting). We then re-take the pressures about every 4 weeks as the LOP may change depending on if the limb is getting bigger or smaller and how the body is adapting to BFR.

Establishing LOP Automatically with the consumer version of SmartCuffs:

If you are using an automated pump and doppler, the process is much simpler than the manual version. In the SmartCuff consumer version of the pump, when you turn it on by pressing the round button on the right quickly, notice what firmware version you are using. In this case, the firmware is in the lower right corner. If you need to update the firmware, you can choose 'update settings' on the Welcome! Screen.

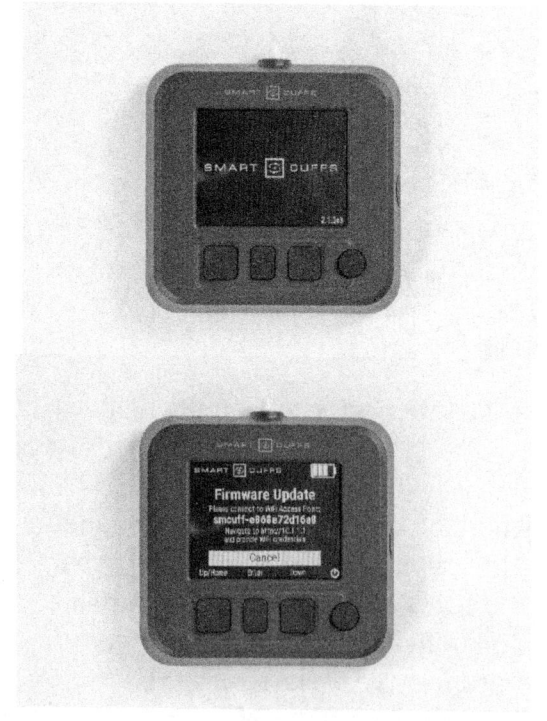

If your firmware is up to date, then proceed to 'Start Exercise' on the Welcome! Screen.

Apply the cuffs to the upper or lower extremities. Make sure the cuff is on as tight as possible before connecting the pump.

You will then choose either arm for upper extremity exercises or leg for lower extremity exercises.

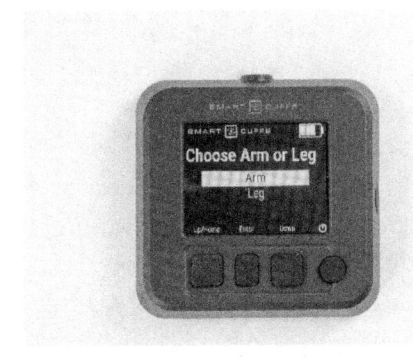

You will then choose your intensity as low, medium or high. Once calibrated you can disconnect and switch over to the other arm. Once inflated you can disconnect the clip and start exercising. With the exercise complete, you can then push the valve on the cuff to deflate the cuff.

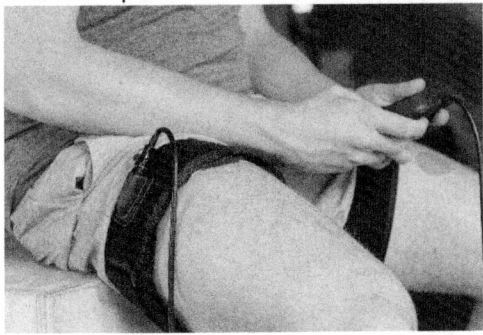

If you are using an automated pump and doppler, the process is much simpler. In the SmartCuff consumer version of the pump, when you turn it on, notice what firmware version you are using. In this case, the firmware is in the lower right corner. If you need to update the firmware, you can choose 'update settings' on the Welcome! Screen.

The consumer version will remember the last pressure you used so when you are ready to reinflate, just push 'last pressure'

Establishing LOP on a client or patient

If you have the SmartCuffs Pro version of the pump there are a few more options and bells and whistles to your disposal. As in the consumer version, make sure are using the most up to date firmware version. Then choose 'start exercise' and choose 'arm' or 'leg'. From here the options are a little different:

Manual – If you already know what pressure you want to exercise at, you can set it here then hit 'enter'. The cuff will automatically inflate to the desired pressure.

Personal Pressure – Choose what % of LOP you want your client/patient to train at. The cuff will automatically inflate to this desired pressure. Once the pump reaches the desired pressure, the LOP will display. I would write down this number for each limb in each body position (sitting, standing and lying down). Then you can calculate your %LOP and use the manual setting (see above) which will be much faster. If time is of the essence (isn't it always in the clinic!), using two pumps at the same time can help with efficiency.

Repeat – Repeats the previous pressure/%LOP

Start New Session – Re-establishes LOP when you switch limbs or go from upper to lower extremities or visa versa

Autoregulate – Keep the pump connected and the pump will maintain the same pressure during the exercise.

IPC – This is short for **I**schemic **P**re/Post **C**onditioning. These are very high pressures 80-100% LOP) we use for exercise recovery or prior to doing performance based high intensity training. We do not exercise with these pressures.

How much weight should I use?

We should be able to perform at least 30 repetitions of an exercise without the cuffs if we want to use that resistance with cuffs. For example, if I can do 30 repetitions of bench press with 100 lbs but can only do 26 repetitions with 110lbs, I will use 100lbs. With body weight exercise, be able to perform 30 repetitions without a rest. For example, if I can only perform 25 straight air squats without rest, this intensity is too much for me so I need to regress the exercise. A way for me to regress the exercise is to use a TRX Suspension Trainer or a door jam to help support my weight.

Using a TRX Suspension Trainer post surgery to help with BFR air squat

Establishing Your Estimated 1 Rep Max (1RM)

In order to establish your estimated k1RM for each exercise we are going to use a chart so we can calculate your 1RM without actually having to spend the time increasing weight until we get to the last weight we can lift one time. We will use the chart below.

Number of repetitions performed	Percentage of 1 repetition maximum	Multiply weight lifted by:
1	100	1.00
2	95	1.05
3	93	1.08
4	90	1.11
5	87	1.15
6	85	1.18
7	83	1.20
8	80	1.25
9	77	1.30
10	75	1.33
11	70	1.43
12	67	1.49
15	65	1.54

Follow this example to calculate your 1RM.
Ken is able to lift 100 lbs x 10 repetitions when performing a shoulder press. By using our chart we see that we would multiple his 10RM by 1.33 giving us a 1RM of 133 lbs.

To the beginning BFR trainee you may want to start with simple exercises to perform. A good starting point would be to start with modified pushups, bicep curls, triceps extension, air squat, and shoulder press. These exercises can give you a good total body workout and start your emersion into BFR training.

Download the 'Getting Started' worksheet at bfruniversity/drlecarasguide

Conclusion

This chapter has given you all of the baseline data you will need to start training with BFR. Training results and protocols will be discussed in other chapters. If I could leave you with these last words of advice for this chapter it would be do not skip these steps before starting to train with BFR. It does not take much time to set up your training correctly and for optimal success if you follow these simple instructions. It can however, cost you time training and time spent not training due to injury if you are not training correctly.

If you cannot measure your limb girth and find the proper limb occlusion pressure alone, then please ask a friend or colleague to help you. Again, do not skip this first, simple step in making sure that your training is the best it can be.

Chapter 8: BFR TRAINING BENEFITS

There are many reasons why one would want to improve muscle mass and strength and why blood flow restriction training is so interesting for a wide variety of individuals. For me, it was knowing under normal circumstances it takes between 12 and 16 weeks in order to build muscle mass and strength and all of a sudden having technology that can provide the same benefit in three to four weeks!

This expedited adaptation while only using very lite loads (between 20 – 35% 1-RM) blew my mind in my early days of discovery. Many people want to improve muscle mass and strength from an early age. An 11-year-old wants to improve his muscle mass and strength to be a better football player. My 87-year-old father wants to improve his muscle mass and strength to make sure that he can do the activities that he wants to do on a daily basis. My dad wants to be strong enough to pick up his grandchildren and great-grandchildren. Everybody and everyone along the age spectrum, young and old, wants to make sure that they have enough muscle mass and strength, although it might be for many different reasons.

In this chapter, I'm going to walk you through some of the benefits of blood flow restriction training. And why it really is effective for nearly the entire population for our health and wellbeing. One of the primary reasons blood flow training has exploded in the United States is because of its ability to increase muscle size. The fancy word for increasing muscle size is hypertrophy.

How do we increase muscle mass? Well, that's to be determined. As an undergrad exercise physiology major, the textbooks, and thus our professors, taught us in order to improve muscle mass, you had to break down the muscle tissue with heavy resistance training. This break down of tissue due to exercise is termed Exercise Induced Muscle Damage abbreviated EIMD. Meaning I had to exercise at a high enough intensity to cause EIMD so my body (and brain) would initiate the process to rebuild the tissue. I wanted to have soreness linger for a day or two, and then rest long enough to allow my body to recover. And the thought process was always, Hey, if I have to sprint and run away from a saber tooth tiger today, I've got to be prepared to run away from that T-rex tomorrow. Otherwise, I might be dinner.

The body needs to repair very, very quickly. And the coolest thing about blood flow restriction training is that it tricks your body and your brain to make these 'repairs' even though there has not been any damage done. That's truly the key. There are many different mechanisms and thoughts about how our bodies adapt. At this point we are not exactly sure how the body repairs but we know there are many different systems in play from the local tissue to the brain involvement, hormones, endocrine system and paracrine system.

There are mechanical tension mechanisms, and they are other mechanisms that we don't even know about yet because this has totally turned the exercise physiology world upside down. Scientists thought they knew why muscle strength and hypertrophy occur, but what we know is we don't really know. And so there are many, many benefits of blood flow restriction training. There are studies every week coming out about blood flow restriction training. I'm going to touch on some of the benefits that I know of and hopefully in the future, I will come out with more benefits as we continue down this road of discovery.

Increased Muscle Size is (Literally) The Biggest Benefit to BFRT

Increased muscle size (hypertrophy) appears to be the biggest benefit of blood flow restriction training. Hypertrophy happens quickly within about three weeks in as little as 2-3 days per week of training. Hypertrophy is beneficial for people with diseases that won't allow them to grow muscle as they should. Hypertrophy is also beneficial for the bodybuilder that has difficulty increasing the size of his calves because genetically his calves just don't want to get big.

Personally, my biceps have never been that big and I love blood flow restriction training because it helps me get that pump and helps me feel like at least I'm on the right path. Muscle mass can be really important too for general health, because muscle is really important. Muscle helps generate force and power. It helps drive movement of the skeletal system and it helps enable function and activity. My grandfather, unfortunately, as he got older preferred to see the rise in his stock prices rather than the rise in his muscle mass and his functional capacity. And as he sat there watching the Dow Jones and the ticker tape increase his overall **wealth**, the resultant inactivity drove down his functional capacity and overall **health**. He lost more and more muscle mass until the point when he couldn't do much for himself and withered away.

Less than 10% of the population older than 75 years of age in the United States participate in muscle strengthening activities. That's a very low percentage considering we now live until we're in our nineties. We need to be increasing muscle mass over time just to generate physical force and power, drive movement, and enable function and activity.

Muscle is very important for your metabolism. It's the primary site of insulin mediated, glucose disposal, meaning sugar. Sugar is built up in your muscle and is stored there to provide energy for the muscle to be active. We use the stored sugar as an energy source to do the activities of daily living. The more muscle we have, the more energy we have that's readily available for us.
Muscle is also the largest reservoir of glycogen in the body. Glycogen is the form of glucose (sugar) that is ready and instantly converted to energy. Lastly, muscle helps us be very resilient. It allows for strength, mobility, and endurance to reduce frailty of our system. It has adaptive capacity for multiple disease states. The loss of muscle mass can be devastating just like it was for my grandfather as he withered away until he finally passed.

Muscle mass is important. It's something that everybody wants to maintain and build, not just for looking good at the beach, but for overall function and quality of life.

Strength is Different Than Hypertrophy

We just talked about hypertrophy in the previous section. Why are we talking separately about strength? Well, believe it or not strength and hypertrophy, although linked are not direct causations. There are many people I know that are pretty big, but are not very strong and vice versa. There are people that you look at who don't look very strong, but they're really strong. Strength training is a different type of a training program than hypertrophy training. It's a different goal to be strong. When I was wrestling in college, I loved wrestling the big bulky guys because they ran out of energy quickly. I hated wrestling the thin sinewy guys because they were strong and built to last.

Ask any wrestler. There are two types of people that short stocky guys, like myself, don't want to wrestle. They are tall skinny guys and they can reach around and grab things that you had no idea that they could grab. These guys don't necessarily have lots of muscle mass, but they are strong. They use their leverage. They can utilize muscle in very effective ways differently than how I do as a short stocky guy.

Strength can be a huge benefit in BFR training. In a recent study I was participating in at the University of Jacksonville in Florida, we saw within four weeks increases in one rep max in both squat and bench press using blood flow restriction training in collegiate football players. I've seen in my clinic is this correlates to people that are rehabbing with me in the clinic and worldwide.

A tertiary benefit of blood flow restriction training is stimulating type two muscle fibers. There are two different types of muscle fibers that we talk about in science. Type one muscle fibers are the ones we use most of the day. They're oxygen based. They help us get around and walk at low intensities and move around. They are not particularly effective in increasing size and strength.

The ones that we want to get to with training are type two fibers. They have greater maximal contraction, velocity, and have higher, maximum power outputs than type one fibers. And in order to be an efficient organism we need to tap into these type two fibers.

In my opinion. The only way to tap into these type two fibers before BFR was high intensity exercise or taking low intensity exercise all the way to failure. But now with BFR, we can tap into these type two fibers by pre-fatiguing type one fibers. We are able to allow those type one fibers to get so tired that in order to continue exercise, you have to use your type two fibers. Those type two fibers are the ones that are going to help us grow, help us be more powerful, and help us be a more efficient organism.

BFR Training Improves Microcirculation

BFR can also improve microcirculation. Microcirculation is the exchange between blood and oxygen. This is vital for healthy tissue. This is vital for aerobic capacity. This is vital to allow us to do the activities that we want to do. Microcirculation gets worse as we get older. We become less efficient at easily using the oxygen that we have. We get less efficient at blowing off carbon dioxide and metabolic byproducts, including those that are toxic. The byproducts accumulate and we can't exercise as long as we we did before when we were younger. BFR, even under low intensity states improves our ability primarily through nitric oxide production, and this allows for more efficient microcirculation, healthier tissue, and improved ability to build new blood vessels.

Another cytokine that is produced with BFR is called vascular endothelial growth factor or VEGF. VEGF is relatively new to the exercise physiology community. VEGF was discovered in 1989 and has really helped us understand this process of building new blood vessels. VEGF helps increase tissue capillary density in response to a lack of oxygen or hypoxic signaling.

Hypoxia is the lack of oxygen. It is a major regulator of VEGF expression through hypoxia, inducible factor one alpha or HIF one alpha. And let's not get too deep into the weeds here. This isn't a book on exercise physiology or biochemistry, but understanding that these systems are complex and overlap, and rely on one another, is important.

Our Body Has Backup Systems to Backup Systems

We have backup systems to backup systems. It's like having six different hard drives for your computer that constantly are getting backed up. If one fails, one kicks in right away. The body is an amazing adaptive organism; more efficient and more effective than any computer you could possibly imagine.

Understanding this is complex and we don't fully understand all the mechanisms yet is okay. What we do know is that by creating an area where there's less oxygen than your body really wants improves the ability to utilize the oxygen that it does has. And VEGF is one of those ways that helps us utilize oxygen, create more blood vessels, and improve the overall health of the tissue.

I mentioned nitric oxide (NO) before, and it's worth mentioning a little bit further. Nitric oxide is an important signaling molecule produced at high levels in muscle by neuronal nitric oxide synthase. BFR increases nitric has been found to stimulate myosatellite or STEM cells. STEM cells are the coolest thing ever.

I mentioned exercise induced muscle damage before. I want to explain why a muscle strain is different than a muscle tear needing surgical repair. In reality, there's not much difference between the two. Muscle tears are just larger holes in the tissue. Think about having a wall and hanging posters on the wall with thumbtacks. When I was a kid I would hang posters on the wall with thumbtacks. I used them because I knew it was easy to repair the thumbtack holes. I could take a little bit of toothpaste and put it over that little hole and toothpaste would fill the hole and it would be easy to paint over. No big deal. Nobody would know the difference.

Think of that little tiny pinprick hole as exercise induced muscle damage. It's a slight breakdown of muscle tissue that your body can easily repair if you give it enough time. It takes between 24 and 48 hours for moderate exercise and 72 to 96 hours for full repair of exercise, induced muscle damage. By the way, that's why our body makes us sore. Soreness is a good thing. I once thought soreness was a bad and I would try to do anything I could to help my athletes stop being sore all the time. I would use things like massage and electric stimulation and heat and NormaTec compression to stop the soreness. But my thinking has been different more recently, viewing soreness as a protective mechanism.

Have you ever noticed when you are super sore, you don't have the normal range of motion that you normally would have? Have you ever noticed that you're not able to lift as much weight? Have we ever thought that there's a reason for that? The reason is your body's trying to protect you from doing the same activity again and progressing that pin prick to a large hole. If you kick the wall, the hole becomes too big. Sometimes the body can't repair it.

I can't repair that hole with toothpaste or spackle. I've got to go to a home repair store and buy mesh. I've got to put mesh or some sort of reinforcement behind the hole in order to make the wall whole again. Mesh is like scar tissue and that wall is never going to be the same again. It's not one continuous wall anymore. There is a patch just like our body has to patch larger and more intense damage to the tissue.

Where does STEM cell come into all this? STEM cells are these cool little cells that sit on the outside of muscle. When we have small amounts of damage to the muscle, it activates these STEM cells. STEM cells go down in pairs. One fills (toothpaste) and one reproduces the cell. These cells will reproduce and share their nucleus with the muscle cell so that muscle cell then can increase the size. Increasing the size increases the repair, and make the tissue whole again.

What if you were able to make more of that spackle or that toothpaste to repair the tissue without the need for surgery or other fancy, medical devices or procedures? Well, BFR increases satellite STEM cell production. I see this in the clinic all the time. Something that I think is probably going to need PRP or shockwave therapy to help the muscle STEM cell to repair the tissue can be repaired just by using BFR in a normal rehab setting.

As we get older, we reduce the amount of satellite cells availability. This is one reason as we get older it seems harder to recover from intense exercise. Just getting older, reduces our ability for our bodies to repair the tissue that we damage with normal exercise and activities. Once I hit 40 years old, I can't tell you how sore I am all the time, doing activity and not doing any activity. It's so frustrating. And I hear the same thing from my patients on a daily basis. This must just be me getting old because 10 years ago, I would have this pain for a day and then it would just go away. Well, there is some truth to that. Age does make us less effective. Age does reduce the amount of hormone circulating through the body. Age does reduce the amount of STEM cells available, but we can reverse it.

Don't be part of that 8.7% of the population that actually lifts weights. Be like my parents who are in their eighties, lifting weights three times a week. To make sure they maintain their muscle mass they use BFR because we can still use those light loads, not cause any damage to the tissue, and still get the benefits of high intensity exercise.

That's what gives me chills about BFR as I sit here and write this. That's what gives me hope. As we get older and we learn to live longer, we can do so better. We don't have to live like grandfather sitting in a chair and withering away. We can be more productive and live our best life.

BFR can be very beneficial for mitochondrial production. Mitochondria help regulate muscle metabolism and mitochondrial dysfunction plays a major role in inflammation and the progression of sarcopenia. Mitochondria are the little nuclear plants in our cells. Mitochondria help our energy systems and they can be improved and increased using BFR.

BFR Training Without Exercise is Beneficial

BFR appears to help by reducing the amount of oxygen in the tissue. BFR without exercise can be beneficial by just reducing the amount of oxygen, putting a little stress into the system, and allowing the body to adapt to that stress. When we have too much of anything, we as humans, don't do very well. Think about all those lottery winners who get all this money. Many lottery winners blow it. They spend it and they end up more broke than they were before they won the lottery. Our bodies are the same way.

What happens when we give our body too much of anything? What happens when we give our body just slightly less than what it wants? You give it just a little bit of stress. That's where this big intermittent fasting phenomenon has come from the last few years, even though it's been around for a long time, intermittent fasting has been shown to be very beneficial for the human organism because we're slightly depriving our bodies of what it needs (food).

Our bodies thrive when we are deprived just a little bit. Same principle with exercise. Too much exercise causes damage. Too little exercise doesn't do anything. Our body doesn't have to adapt. Just the right amount of exercise allows our body to be constantly stimulated and improve our overall capacity. Always think about that when you're doing any type of exercise. We're trying to give the body what it wants in order to preserve itself. Other things like growth hormone and insulin growth factor have been shown to be increased with blood flow restriction training. And these are vital mechanisms for the overall health of our muscle and our systems.

BFR Increases Bone Density

There appears to be an increase in bone density when we use blood flow restriction training by stimulating the bone through a lack of oxygen and stimulation of Growth Hormone (GH). It is a strong hormonal stimulus on bony metabolism through increases in growth, hormone, and increases in insulin growth factor one. BFR also activates hypoxia, induce transcription factor, or HIF, thereby increasing the expression of vascular endothelial growth factor, VGF, and the formation of micro-blood vessels in bone tissue.

BFR could be a total game changer for those with osteoporosis and osteopenia, for improving the ability to maintain muscle mass as we age, and to improve the overall health of the human organism.

Aerobic Capacity:

We can use BFR to improve our aerobic capacity. There have been numerous studies looking at low intensity walking or cycling and the improvement in aerobic fitness measured via V02 Max. The other interesting component of this is if you use BFR for walking, you also get increased muscle size and strength in the thigh. (Ozaki, 2011; Abe, 2010) Some researchers would say this increased muscle size and strength should also help reduce the risk of fall in older individuals. But older individuals are not the only ones who benefit from this type of aerobic training. High level Division I basketball players also benefited from 2/day walking with BFR for 15 minutes at low speeds. (Park 2010). The basketball players increased their Vo2max by nearly 12%! Pretty incredible that just by walking these athletes can increase their aerobic capacity.

Chapter 9: BFR BASELINES & PROTOCOLS

AEROBIC CAPACITY

One of the coolest protocols that we have for blood flow restriction training is aerobic capacity training. And the reason that I think it's so cool is that not only can you improve your ability to utilize oxygen, but you can increase your aerobic capacity fitness and at the same time increase strength. Numerous studies placed the BFR cuffs on the upper leg, and then had individuals walk, just walk, nothing too aggressive. I'm going to explain how aggressive you need to be walking, but it's very light walking.

You can do these one or two times per day, and it's been shown across the continuum from young athletes, division I basketball players, all the way up to the elderly that by using BFR and a walk protocol, you can increase your aerobic capacity. You can increase strength of the lower extremity and size as well.

If you are a rehab specialist and you have somebody that cannot walk as long as they would like to, whether that's because of prior stroke, lower back problems, radiculopathy, or diabetic neuropathy. You want to improve their function and improve their ability to live their life.

I remember one patient I had named John, and he had had a stroke. He said to me, son, there's two things that I want to be able to do that I cannot currently do. I want to be able to take my dogs for a 15 to 20 minute walk, which I currently can't do without feeling like I'm going to stumble and fall. And number two is I want to be able to go quail hunting with my friends in South Texas. I asked him how long he could currently walk without feeling like he was going to fall. He could walk for about 3 minutes. He had fallen a few times.

We started with BFR on the treadmill so he could use his hands and he would grasp the sides of the treadmill, and we started off at a very light pressure. We did three minutes. Then he would hold on for one minute and then he would do three minutes without holding on. We kept alternating and we slowly built him up until he could walk for 25 minutes without holding on. And to me, that's a total change in somebody's life to improve their functional capacity that way.

And John was really happy with his result and it happened really, really quickly. And he didn't have to walk very fast. He didn't have to walk more than once or twice a day. But we just had to do it. And so we were able to change his aerobic capacity. We were able to increase the strength and size of his legs so he could have a more functional lifestyle.

And that's what BFR Training is all about! It's about being able to utilize technology to trick the brain and trick the body into thinking you're doing more intense exercise than you really are. It allows you to work hard and not cause any muscle damage or any other damage to tissue.

We were able to start this case on a treadmill, but there's some people that can't even get on a treadmill or go for a walk. In that case we could start them on a bike or an elliptical. We could start them on a rowing machine. We have protocols for all different types of modalities. Personally, I think when I'm trying to improve somebody's aerobic capacity, I want to do it in a way that's as functional for that person as possible. I like to start people out walking with BFR Training, but there are always alternatives.

BASELINE MEASUREMENTS

We must first calculate how intense we need to walk and we'll use our heart rate. Heart rate is an easy thing to measure. You can use a heart rate monitor. You probably already have one on your smart phone or smart watch. You can use numerous modalities to know how intense your body is working by measuring your heart rate. For this we are going to use a calculation called the heart rate reserve, and we're going to use this because we don't need a fancy machine or fancy science lab in order to calculate your volume of oxygen, maximum volume of oxygen, or your VO2 max. We're going to use HRR or heart rate reserve as a proxy to our VO2 max. It's a really easy calculation. First, we need to know is your age. That shouldn't be too hard to get.

220 – Age = Estimated Max HR (MHR)

The second component of the equation is a little more complicated. However, it is still easy enough to get. You need your lowest heart rate from throughout the day. Now, normally this is going to be your lowest heart rate in the middle of the night. I wear something called an oura ring that measures my sleep and my heart rate. This allows me to look on my phone and I can find out my lowest heart rate from overnighT. Mine is about 52 beats per minute. Now, if you don't have any of these modalities just measure your heart rate when you first wake up. Before you get out of bed, calculate your heart rate from your carotid artery up by your neck for one minute use a stopwatch or clock. That's your resting heart rate.

Heart Rate upon immediately waking in the morning = Resting Heart Rate (RHR)

Now, we have your estimated MHR and RHR. The last thing that we need is to get your heart rate reserve (HRH). Take your estimated maximum heart rate and subtract your resting heart rate.

MHR – RHR =Heart Rate Reserve (HRR)
220 – 40 AGE = 180 MHR
180 – 52 RHR = 128
HRR = 128

And you're going to multiply the resultant number by 0.30.

128 X .30 = 38.4

That number is going to be the percentage of your heart rate reserve, that we are going to use to start exercising. Then you take that number and add your resting heart rate to get the number that you're going to aim for while you're going for a walk.

%HRR + RHR = Training Zone
38 + 52 = 90
Training Zone = 90 bpm

Most people are going to be between 95 to 110 with the variables being your age and how fit you are. The more fit you are, the lower your resting heart rate Is going to be for most people.

GETTING STARTED

Now that we've got all the numbers down; the next step is putting the cuffs on. Inflate to 60% of your arterial occlusion pressure, but no less than 130mmHg. Then, go for a walk. Adjust your speed or incline until you reach the desired training zone, and walk for 20 minutes. What if you can't walk for 20 minutes? Then walk for 10 minutes. If you can't walk for 10 minutes, then walk for five or whatever you can do. The important thing is to get started wherever your fitness level allows. Your body will begin to accommodate to your training and you will be able to increase your time as you become more fit. You can also do this 2/day. Twice per day training will effectively increase your aerobic capacity quicker.

If you can't do five minutes or more, then it might be best to start on the treadmill. By starting on the treadmill you can take breaks as you need them. You can step off to the sides of the treadmill and give yourself a little bit of break. Move forward and keep going, but we want to try to build up so that you're at 20 minutes of aerobic exercise. You would follow this method the exact same way if you are starting on a bike. And the thing that you'll play around with is the resistance or your cadence. On the bike, maintain 70 revolutions per minute. Then, slightly increase the resistance every minute until you get to your target heart rate. On the treadmill, set the incline to 1. . That's been shown to be the equivalent to walking outside with wind resistance. Then, increase the speed by .5 every minute until you get to your target heart rate.

TRAINING FREQUENCY

How often do we need to train to see the maximum benefits? Some studies have shown doing it twice a day. A study with division I basketball players showed an increase in VO2 max by up to 12% within just 2 weeks with 2/day training. If you're in a rush to get into better shape due to coming off and injury and you're wanting to get back into the field, then you may want to train twice a day to speed up your return to play. Each session would be 15-20 minutes. If you're in it for the long haul and you're just getting back to exercising after a long layoff then once a day for 20 minutes would be great. No less than five times a week is what I'm going to recommend at these low intensities. There are high intensity protocols, but I'm going to reserve those for a different book because this is really the beginner's book on blood flow restriction training.

For more information, you can look at my performance course by going to smart toolsplus.com under education and you can see protocols outside of a basic or rehab setting, There are other protocols that we can use to increase size, strength, and aerobic capacity.

REPS, SETS AND FREQUENCY

The general consensus is most BFR resistance exercise sessions should consist of between 3-5 exercises. Each exercise is performed for 30 repetitions, rest 30 seconds, 15 repetitions, 30 second rest, 15 repetitions, 30 second rest, 15 repetitions then deflate the cuffs. This is 75 repetitions total. Repetitions should be performed slowly (2 second contraction, 0 rest at top and 2 second eccentric). The repetitions intensity should be like this...

Set 1
Rep 1 - Easy
Rep 2 - Easy
Rep 3 - Easy
Rep 4 - Easy
Rep 5 - Easy
Rep 6 – Easy
Rep 7 – Easy
Rep 8 – Easy
Rep 9 – Easy
Rep 10 – Easy
Rep 1 - Easy
Rep 12 - Easy
Rep 13 - Easy
Rep 14 - Easy
Rep 15 - Easy
Rep 16 – Easy
Rep 17 – Easy
Rep 18 – Easy
Rep 19 – Easy
Rep 20 – Easy
Rep 21 - Easy
Rep 22 - Easy
Rep 23 - Easy
Rep 24 - Easy
Rep 25 - Easy
Rep 26 – Easy
Rep 27 – Easy
Rep 28 – Easy

Rep 29 – Easy
Rep 30 – Easy

Take a 30 second rest but keep the cuffs inflated. Put the weights down.

Set 2
Rep 1 - Easy
Rep 2 - Easy
Rep 3 - Easy
Rep 4 - Easy
Rep 5 - Easy
Rep 6 – Easy
Rep 7 – Easy
Rep 8 – Getting a bit difficult
Rep 9 – Getting a bit difficult
Rep 10 – Getting a bit difficult
Rep 1 - Getting a bit difficult
Rep 12 - Getting a bit difficult
Rep 13 – Feeling like you want to get done
Rep 14 - Feeling like you want to get done
Rep 15 – Thank goodness this is my last rep and I get a break

Take a 30 second rest but keep the cuffs inflated. Put the weights down.

Set 3
Rep 1 - Easy
Rep 2 - Easy
Rep 3 - Easy
Rep 4 - Easy
Rep 5 - Easy

Rep 6 – Easy
Rep 7 – Easy
Rep 8 – Getting a bit difficult
Rep 9 – Getting a bit difficult
Rep 10 – Getting a bit difficult
Rep 1 - Getting a bit difficult
Rep 12 - Getting a bit difficult
Rep 13 – Feeling like you want to get done
Rep 14 - Feeling like you want to get done
Rep 15 – Thank goodness this is my last rep and I get a break

Take a 30 second rest but keep the cuffs inflated. Put the weights down.

Set 4
Rep 1 - Moderate
Rep 2 - Moderate
Rep 3 - Moderate
Rep 4 – Getting harder
Rep 5 – Getting harder
Rep 6 – Wanting to rush!
Rep 7 – Wanting to rush!
Rep 8 – difficult
Rep 9 – difficult
Rep 10 – difficult
Rep 1 - difficult
Rep 12 - difficult
Rep 13 – Not sure I can finish
Rep 14 – OMG, OMG, OMG!
Rep 15 – Thank goodness this is my last rep and I get a break!!

Put the weights down and GET THESE CUFFS OFF!!

You would then take a 1-minute break and then move on to the next exercise.

If this is not how the exercise is feeling, the weight is probably a bit too light. Next time you perform this exercise, increase the weight. I would keep a journal to record your progress. If you cannot complete the entire 75 repetitions, then the weight is too high. Drop the weight down. The exertion should be about a 7/10. You will sweat. It is difficult if done correctly.

For example, I want to do an upper body pull day. I would perform latissimus (lat) pulldowns, horizontal rows, then dumbbell bicep curls. If you still have something left in the tank then hammer curls would be a good idea.

For a video of how this looks, please go to
www.bfruniversity.com/bfrbook/repsandsets

WHAT ARE THE EXACT MECHANISMS BEHIND BFR TRAINING?

The answer is that we don't exactly know. There are numerous mechanisms that we've talked about before. And we're not totally sure what the exact mechanisms are at the cellular level. Things are happening at the brain and things are happening at the muscle. They all work together and I'm not smart enough to be able to dissect exactly what the body and brain and cells are all doing. But our body is pretty smart and it will adapt if we give it just enough stress and just enough rest. Again, the cool thing about blood flow restriction training is if you do it the way that I'm prescribing there is no muscle damage. We can do it multiple times a day without risk of having enough rest between sessions.

Start aerobic capacity training five days a week and you'll see drastic changes over a short amount of time. I recommend re-evaluating your heart rate reserve after about four weeks. I also recommend re-evaluating your one rep max, because you're going to get stronger. And if you get stronger, your one rep max is no longer your one rep max. It's gone up! Recalculate every so often so you can insure that your training appropriately and improve your fitness. Heart rate reserve will change as well. You should see a drop in your resting heart rate which will change your exercise intensity needed to meet your ideal training zone.

CARDIAC OUTPUT

Cardiac output is the amount of blood that gets pushed through the atrium on every beat or every heartbeat. It has two components; stroke volume and frequency. Stroke volume is the amount of fluid that's actually leaving the heart. The frequency is the speed your heart is beating or your heart rate. Cardiac output is equal to heart rate times stroke volume.

$$CO = HR \times SV$$

When we use cuffs, we are eliminating the Venus return back to the heart, which in layman's terms means that we're reducing your stroke volume. You have less fluid flowing because everything away from the cuff is getting trapped. You're losing that volume. In order to maintain the same cardiac output, your heart rate has to increase. This is where most experts believe the largest benefits of aerobic capacity training with BFR is altering that cardiac output by reducing stroke volume and forcing your heart to work a little bit harder.

FINAL MECHANISMS

Other things that happen, which we've talked about before is the hypoxia effect or the lack of oxygen due to a decrease in blood flow to the working limbs. Vascular endothelial growth factor appears to play a large role in BFR Training. Also, insulin growth factor appears to play a large role locally at the tissue. If we're creating a hypoxic event, then we're increasing vascular endothelial growth facto and other factors that improve the micro vascularization or the exchange of oxygen in the blood to the muscle. We think that that hypoxic environment improves your ability to utilize the oxygen in the muscle itself. Lastly, lactate production appears to also play a beneficial role. The better that we are able to tolerate an acidic environment or an exercised acidosis, the more tolerant our body will be towards aerobic capacity training and high intensity training with or without BFR cuffs.

The body is a phenomenal thing. We give it just enough stress and it will adapt. We give it too much stress and it gets injured. The goal of all your health coaches, physical therapists, chiropractors, and physicians is to coach you on how to give you just enough stress without injuring yourself and how to improve your aerobic and functional capacity over time in order to improve your life and allow you to do the things that you want to do until it's time for you to meet your maker.

PROGRAMMING FOR GENERAL FITNESS:

Monday

Morning:	20-minute BFR walk at 35% HRR and 60% LOP
Afternoon:	Upper Body Push at 20%1RM and 40% LOP
	Modified Push-up
	Banded triceps push-down
	Dumbbell Shoulder Press

Tuesday

Morning:	20-minute BFR walk at 35% HRR and 60% LOP
Afternoon:	Lower Body at 20%1RM and 60% LOP
	Chair Squats
	Leg Extensions
	Standing Hamstring Curls

Wednesday

Morning:	20-minute BFR walk at 35% HRR and 60% LOP

Thursday

Morning:	20-minute BFR walk at 35% HRR and 60% LOP
Afternoon:	Upper Body Pull at 20%1RM and 40% LOP
	Lat Pull Down

Horizontal Row
Bicep Curl

Friday
Morning: 20-minute BFR walk at 35% HRR and 60% LOP
Afternoon: Lower Body at 20%1RM and 60% LOP
Glute Bridges
Leg Extensions
Standing Hamstring Curls

Saturday

Morning: 20-minute BFR walk at 35% HRR and 60% LOP
Afternoon: Upper Body Push at 20%1RM and 40% LOP
Bench Press
Dumbbell Skull Crushers
Dumbbell Lateral Raises

A word about going to failure. It is absolutely okay to go to failure during the last set of 15 reps. Just be aware you will be more sore the next day and will require more rest before your next session of the same body regions. You can increase your % of LOP by 5% per week until you reach the max of 50% in the upper extremity and 80% in the lower extremity although in the lower extremity I am not convinced it is necessary to go above 60% LOP as long as 60% is above 130mmHg.

If you don't want to walk everyday you can exchange walking with any hamster wheel activity your like (stairmaster, treadmill, elliptical or bicycle).

*all exercises are performed at 30 reps, 15 reps, 15 reps, 15 reps then deflate for 1 minute. Proceed to next exercise.

Chapter 10: EXERCISES FOR BFR

Here are some examples of exercises that can be done using light loads with BFR. Of course, there are endless ways to create resistance....dumbbells, kettlebells, body weight, barbells, resistance bands, etc. You can pretty much do any exercise you like.

I like to separate Upper body push, Upper body pulls, Hip Dominant, Knee Dominant, core and and ancillary.

Upper Body Push Exercises

BFR Bench Press – can also be done with dumbbells

BFR Incline Bench Press – Can also be performed with a barbell

BFR Modified Push Up

BFR Barbell Shoulder to overhead. Can also be performed with dumbbells or kettlebells or resistance bands

BFR Dumbbell Shoulder to overhead. Can also be done with kettlebells or barbell

Upper Body Pull Exercises

BFR DB Bent over Rows. Can also use a barbell

BFR Horizontal Rows

BFR Latissimus Pulldown

Ancillary Exercises

BFR barbell bicep curl – can also be done with dumbbells

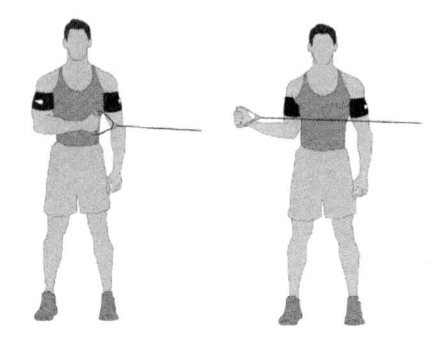

BFR Shoulder External Rotation

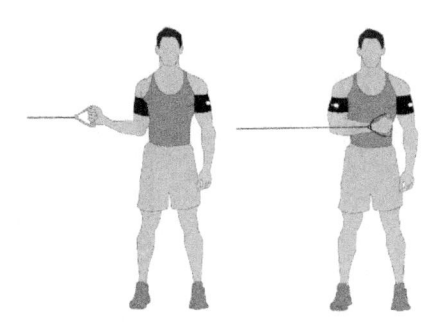

BFR Shoulder internal rotation

BFR Skull Crushers – Can also be performed with dumbbells

BFR Tricep Extensions – Can also be done with a resistance band

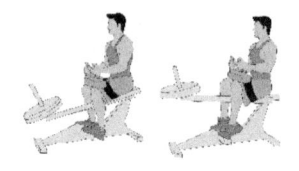

BFR Bent Knee Calf Raises – Can also be done seated with dumbbells on your knees. This exercise is good for the soleus muscle in the calf. This muscle adds size to the calf.

BFR Straight Legged Calf Raises – Good for the outer calf muscle called the gastrocnemius which is good for developing definition

Lower Body

Hip Dominate Exercises

BFR Back squat – Can also be performed as an air squat or with dumbells

BFR Lunges – weight can be added by holding dumbbells, kettlebells or a barbell to the front rack position or high on the back

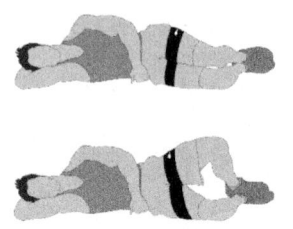

BFR Clam Shells – If you need some resistance, use an 18" elastic resistance around your legs, just above your knees

Knee Dominant Exercises

BFR Prone Hamstring Curls – Can also be done lying face down (prone) and using ankle weights

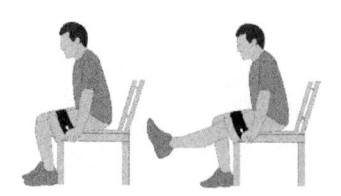

BFR Long Arc Quad – This the alternative exercise to quadricep extensions (see below)

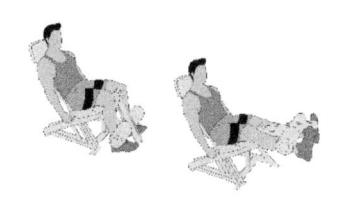

BFR Long Arc Quad – Can also be performed with or without ankle weights. This exercise is good for the front muscles of the leg.

BFR Standing Hamstring Curls – Can also be done lying on a ham curl machine or use ankle weights and support yourself on a counter.

Chapter 11: AEROBIC TRAINING:

BFR can be used on nearly any device you like from treadmills to stair climbers to elliptical.

BFR Cycling

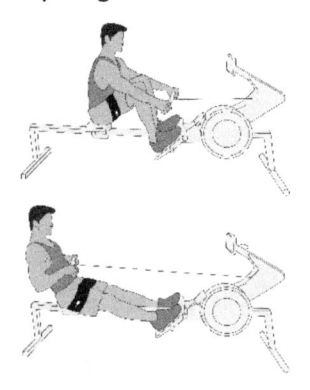

BFR Rowing – Cuffs are normally worn on the legs. The cuffs can be worn on the arms but the heart rate will get very high, very quickly.

BFR Running

BFR Swimming – Cuffs are normally worn on the legs but can be worn on the arms.

BFR Treadmill Walking or Running

References

Dankel, S. J., Buckner, S. L., Jessee, M. B., Mattocks, K. T., Mouser, J. G., Counts, B. R., . . . Loenneke, J. P. (2018). Can blood flow restriction augment muscle activation during high-load training? *Clin Physiol Funct Imaging, 38*(2), 291-295. doi:10.1111/cpf.12414

Downs, M. E., Hackney, K. J., Martin, D., Caine, T. L., Cunningham, D., O'Connor, D. P., & Ploutz-Snyder, L. L. (2014). Acute vascular and cardiovascular responses to blood flow-restricted exercise. *Medicine and science in sports and exercise, 46*(8), 1489-1497.

Global, K. Retrieved from https://www.kaatsu-global.com/index.cfm?Action=About.Home#History

Goldberg, A. L., Etlinger, J. D., Goldspink, D. F., & Jablecki, C. (1975). Mechanism of work-induced hypertrophy of skeletal muscle. *Medicine and science in sports, 7*(3), 185-198.

Henneman, E., Somjen, G., & Carpenter, D. O. (1965). FUNCTIONAL SIGNIFICANCE OF CELL SIZE IN SPINAL MOTONEURONS. *Journal of neurophysiology, 28*, 560-580.

Hylden, C., Burns, T., Stinner, D., & Owens, J. (2015). Blood flow restriction rehabilitation for extremity weakness: a case series. *J Spec Oper Med, 15*(1), 50-56.

Jessee, M. B., Mattocks, K. T., S.L., B., Dankel, S. J., Mouser, J. G., Abe, T., & Loenneke, J. P. (2018). Mechanisms of Blood Flow Restriction: The New Testament. *Techniques in Orthopaedics, Volume Publish Ahead of Print.*

Kraemer, W. J., Marchitelli, L., Gordon, S. E., Harman, E., Dziados, J. E., Mello, R., . . . Fleck, S. J. (1990). Hormonal and growth factor responses to heavy resistance exercise protocols. *Journal of applied physiology (Bethesda, Md. : 1985), 69*(4), 1442-1450.

Liu, Y., Vertommen, D., Rider, M. H., & Lai, Y.-C. (2013). Mammalian target of rapamycin-independent S6K1 and 4E-BP1 phosphorylation during contraction in rat skeletal muscle. *Cellular signalling, 25*(9), 1877-1886.

Loenneke, J. P., Fahs, C. A., Rossow, L. M., Thiebaud, R. S., Mattocks, K. T., Abe, T., & Bemben, M. G. (2013). Blood flow restriction pressure recommendations: a tale of two cuffs. *Frontiers in physiology, 4*, 249.

Loenneke, J. P., Wilson, G. J., & Wilson, J. M. (2010). A mechanistic approach to blood flow occlusion. *Int J Sports Med, 31*(1), 1-4. doi:10.1055/s-0029-1239499

MacDougall, J. D., Sale, D. G., Elder, G. C., & Sutton, J. R. (1982). Muscle ultrastructural characteristics of elite powerlifters and bodybuilders. *European journal of applied physiology and occupational physiology, 48*(1), 117-126.

Manini, T. M., & Clark, B. C. (2009). Blood flow restricted exercise and skeletal muscle health. *Exercise and sport sciences reviews, 37*(2), 78-85.

McCall, G. E., Byrnes, W. C., Dickinson, A., Pattany, P. M., & Fleck, S. J. (1996). Muscle fiber hypertrophy, hyperplasia, and capillary density in college men after resistance training. *Journal of applied physiology (Bethesda, Md. : 1985), 81*(5), 2004-2012.

Owens, J. (2016). *Blood Flow Restriction Rehabilitation*.

Patterson, S., Hughes, L., Warmington, S., Burr, J., Scott, B., Owens, J., . . . Loenneke, J. (2019). Blood Flow Restriction Exercise Position Stand: Considerations of Methodology, Application, and Safety. *Frontiers in Physiology, 10*, 533.

Pearson, S. J., & Hussain, S. R. (2015). A review on the mechanisms of blood-flow restriction resistance training-induced muscle hypertrophy. *Sports Med, 45*(2), 187-200. doi:10.1007/s40279-014-0264-9

Scott, B. R., Loenneke, J. P., Slattery, K. M., & Dascombe, B. J. (2015). Exercise with blood flow restriction: an updated evidence-based approach for enhanced muscular development. *Sports Med, 45*(3), 313-325. doi:10.1007/s40279-014-0288-1

Scott, B. R., Slattery, K. M., Sculley, D. V., & Dascombe, B. J. (2014). Hypoxia and resistance exercise: a comparison of localized and systemic methods. *Sports Med, 44*(8), 1037-1054. doi:10.1007/s40279-014-0177-7

Vandenburgh, H., & Kaufman, S. (1979). In vitro model for stretch-induced hypertrophy of skeletal muscle. *Science (New York, N.Y.), 203*(4377), 265-268.

References

Dankel, S. J., Buckner, S. L., Jessee, M. B., Mattocks, K. T., Mouser, J. G., Counts, B. R., . . . Loenneke, J. P. (2018). Can blood flow restriction augment muscle activation during high-load training? *Clin Physiol Funct Imaging, 38*(2), 291-295. doi:10.1111/cpf.12414

Downs, M. E., Hackney, K. J., Martin, D., Caine, T. L., Cunningham, D., O'Connor, D. P., & Ploutz-Snyder, L. L. (2014). Acute vascular and cardiovascular responses to blood flow-restricted exercise. *Medicine and science in sports and exercise, 46*(8), 1489-1497.

Global, K. Retrieved from https://www.kaatsu-global.com/index.cfm?Action=About.Home#History

Goldberg, A. L., Etlinger, J. D., Goldspink, D. F., & Jablecki, C. (1975). Mechanism of work-induced hypertrophy of skeletal muscle. *Medicine and science in sports, 7*(3), 185-198.

Henneman, E., Somjen, G., & Carpenter, D. O. (1965). FUNCTIONAL SIGNIFICANCE OF CELL SIZE IN SPINAL MOTONEURONS. *Journal of neurophysiology, 28*, 560-580.

Hylden, C., Burns, T., Stinner, D., & Owens, J. (2015). Blood flow restriction rehabilitation for extremity weakness: a case series. *J Spec Oper Med, 15*(1), 50-56.

Jessee, M. B., Mattocks, K. T., S.L., B., Dankel, S. J., Mouser, J. G., Abe, T., & Loenneke, J. P. (2018). Mechanisms of Blood Flow Restriction: The New Testament. *Techniques in Orthopaedics, Volume Publish Ahead of Print*.

Kraemer, W. J., Marchitelli, L., Gordon, S. E., Harman, E., Dziados, J. E., Mello, R., . . . Fleck, S. J. (1990). Hormonal and growth factor responses to heavy resistance exercise protocols. *Journal of applied physiology (Bethesda, Md. : 1985), 69*(4), 1442-1450.

Liu, Y., Vertommen, D., Rider, M. H., & Lai, Y.-C. (2013). Mammalian target of rapamycin-independent S6K1 and 4E-BP1 phosphorylation during contraction in rat skeletal muscle. *Cellular signalling, 25*(9), 1877-1886.

Loenneke, J. P., Fahs, C. A., Rossow, L. M., Thiebaud, R. S., Mattocks, K. T., Abe, T., & Bemben, M. G. (2013). Blood flow restriction pressure recommendations: a tale of two cuffs. *Frontiers in physiology, 4*, 249.

Loenneke, J. P., Wilson, G. J., & Wilson, J. M. (2010). A mechanistic approach to blood flow occlusion. *Int J Sports Med, 31*(1), 1-4. doi:10.1055/s-0029-1239499

MacDougall, J. D., Sale, D. G., Elder, G. C., & Sutton, J. R. (1982). Muscle ultrastructural characteristics of elite powerlifters and bodybuilders. *European journal of applied physiology and occupational physiology, 48*(1), 117-126.

Manini, T. M., & Clark, B. C. (2009). Blood flow restricted exercise and skeletal muscle health. *Exercise and sport sciences reviews, 37*(2), 78-85.

McCall, G. E., Byrnes, W. C., Dickinson, A., Pattany, P. M., & Fleck, S. J. (1996). Muscle fiber hypertrophy, hyperplasia, and capillary density in college men after resistance training. *Journal of applied physiology (Bethesda, Md. : 1985), 81*(5), 2004-2012.

Owens, J. (2016). *Blood Flow Restriction Rehabilitation*.

Patterson, S., Hughes, L., Warmington, S., Burr, J., Scott, B., Owens, J., . . . Loenneke, J. (2019). Blood Flow Restriction Exercise Position Stand: Considerations of Methodology, Application, and Safety. *Frontiers in Physiology, 10*, 533.

Pearson, S. J., & Hussain, S. R. (2015). A review on the mechanisms of blood-flow restriction resistance training-induced muscle hypertrophy. *Sports Med, 45*(2), 187-200. doi:10.1007/s40279-014-0264-9

Scott, B. R., Loenneke, J. P., Slattery, K. M., & Dascombe, B. J. (2015). Exercise with blood flow restriction: an updated evidence-based approach for enhanced muscular development. *Sports Med, 45*(3), 313-325. doi:10.1007/s40279-014-0288-1

Scott, B. R., Slattery, K. M., Sculley, D. V., & Dascombe, B. J. (2014). Hypoxia and resistance exercise: a comparison of localized and systemic methods. *Sports Med, 44*(8), 1037-1054. doi:10.1007/s40279-014-0177-7

Vandenburgh, H., & Kaufman, S. (1979). In vitro model for stretch-induced hypertrophy of skeletal muscle. *Science (New York, N.Y.), 203*(4377), 265-268.

References

Dankel, S. J., Buckner, S. L., Jessee, M. B., Mattocks, K. T., Mouser, J. G., Counts, B. R., . . . Loenneke, J. P. (2018). Can blood flow restriction augment muscle activation during high-load training? *Clin Physiol Funct Imaging, 38*(2), 291-295. doi:10.1111/cpf.12414

Downs, M. E., Hackney, K. J., Martin, D., Caine, T. L., Cunningham, D., O'Connor, D. P., & Ploutz-Snyder, L. L. (2014). Acute vascular and cardiovascular responses to blood flow-restricted exercise. *Medicine and science in sports and exercise, 46*(8), 1489-1497.

Global, K. Retrieved from https://www.kaatsu-global.com/index.cfm?Action=About.Home#History

Goldberg, A. L., Etlinger, J. D., Goldspink, D. F., & Jablecki, C. (1975). Mechanism of work-induced hypertrophy of skeletal muscle. *Medicine and science in sports, 7*(3), 185-198.

Henneman, E., Somjen, G., & Carpenter, D. O. (1965). FUNCTIONAL SIGNIFICANCE OF CELL SIZE IN SPINAL MOTONEURONS. *Journal of neurophysiology, 28*, 560-580.

Hylden, C., Burns, T., Stinner, D., & Owens, J. (2015). Blood flow restriction rehabilitation for extremity weakness: a case series. *J Spec Oper Med, 15*(1), 50-56.

Jessee, M. B., Mattocks, K. T., S.L., B., Dankel, S. J., Mouser, J. G., Abe, T., & Loenneke, J. P. (2018). Mechanisms of Blood Flow Restriction: The New Testament. *Techniques in Orthopaedics, Volume Publish Ahead of Print*.

Kraemer, W. J., Marchitelli, L., Gordon, S. E., Harman, E., Dziados, J. E., Mello, R., . . . Fleck, S. J. (1990). Hormonal and growth factor responses to heavy resistance exercise protocols. *Journal of applied physiology (Bethesda, Md. : 1985), 69*(4), 1442-1450.

Liu, Y., Vertommen, D., Rider, M. H., & Lai, Y.-C. (2013). Mammalian target of rapamycin-independent S6K1 and 4E-BP1 phosphorylation during contraction in rat skeletal muscle. *Cellular signalling, 25*(9), 1877-

1886.

Loenneke, J. P., Fahs, C. A., Rossow, L. M., Thiebaud, R. S., Mattocks, K. T., Abe, T., & Bemben, M. G. (2013). Blood flow restriction pressure recommendations: a tale of two cuffs. *Frontiers in physiology, 4*, 249.

Loenneke, J. P., Wilson, G. J., & Wilson, J. M. (2010). A mechanistic approach to blood flow occlusion. *Int J Sports Med, 31*(1), 1-4. doi:10.1055/s-0029-1239499

MacDougall, J. D., Sale, D. G., Elder, G. C., & Sutton, J. R. (1982). Muscle ultrastructural characteristics of elite powerlifters and bodybuilders. *European journal of applied physiology and occupational physiology, 48*(1), 117-126.

Manini, T. M., & Clark, B. C. (2009). Blood flow restricted exercise and skeletal muscle health. *Exercise and sport sciences reviews, 37*(2), 78-85.

McCall, G. E., Byrnes, W. C., Dickinson, A., Pattany, P. M., & Fleck, S. J. (1996). Muscle fiber hypertrophy, hyperplasia, and capillary density in college men after resistance training. *Journal of applied physiology (Bethesda, Md. : 1985), 81*(5), 2004-2012.

Owens, J. (2016). *Blood Flow Restriction Rehabilitation*.

Patterson, S., Hughes, L., Warmington, S., Burr, J., Scott, B., Owens, J., . . . Loenneke, J. (2019). Blood Flow Restriction Exercise Position Stand: Considerations of Methodology, Application, and Safety. *Frontiers in Physiology, 10*, 533.

Pearson, S. J., & Hussain, S. R. (2015). A review on the mechanisms of blood-flow restriction resistance training-induced muscle hypertrophy. *Sports Med, 45*(2), 187-200. doi:10.1007/s40279-014-0264-9

Scott, B. R., Loenneke, J. P., Slattery, K. M., & Dascombe, B. J. (2015). Exercise with blood flow restriction: an updated evidence-based approach for enhanced muscular development. *Sports Med, 45*(3), 313-325. doi:10.1007/s40279-014-0288-1

Scott, B. R., Slattery, K. M., Sculley, D. V., & Dascombe, B. J. (2014). Hypoxia and resistance exercise: a comparison of localized and systemic methods. *Sports Med, 44*(8), 1037-1054. doi:10.1007/s40279-014-0177-7

Vandenburgh, H., & Kaufman, S. (1979). In vitro model for stretch-induced hypertrophy of skeletal muscle. *Science (New York, N.Y.), 203*(4377), 265-268.

References

Dankel, S. J., Buckner, S. L., Jessee, M. B., Mattocks, K. T., Mouser, J. G., Counts, B. R., . . . Loenneke, J. P. (2018). Can blood flow restriction augment muscle activation during high-load training? *Clin Physiol Funct Imaging, 38*(2), 291-295. doi:10.1111/cpf.12414

Downs, M. E., Hackney, K. J., Martin, D., Caine, T. L., Cunningham, D., O'Connor, D. P., & Ploutz-Snyder, L. L. (2014). Acute vascular and cardiovascular responses to blood flow-restricted exercise. *Medicine and science in sports and exercise, 46*(8), 1489-1497.

Global, K. Retrieved from https://www.kaatsu-global.com/index.cfm?Action=About.Home#History

Goldberg, A. L., Etlinger, J. D., Goldspink, D. F., & Jablecki, C. (1975). Mechanism of work-induced hypertrophy of skeletal muscle. *Medicine and science in sports, 7*(3), 185-198.

Henneman, E., Somjen, G., & Carpenter, D. O. (1965). FUNCTIONAL SIGNIFICANCE OF CELL SIZE IN SPINAL MOTONEURONS. *Journal of neurophysiology, 28*, 560-580.

Hylden, C., Burns, T., Stinner, D., & Owens, J. (2015). Blood flow restriction rehabilitation for extremity weakness: a case series. *J Spec Oper Med, 15*(1), 50-56.

Jessee, M. B., Mattocks, K. T., S.L., B., Dankel, S. J., Mouser, J. G., Abe, T., & Loenneke, J. P. (2018). Mechanisms of Blood Flow Restriction: The New Testament. *Techniques in Orthopaedics, Volume Publish Ahead of Print.*

Kraemer, W. J., Marchitelli, L., Gordon, S. E., Harman, E., Dziados, J. E., Mello, R., . . . Fleck, S. J. (1990). Hormonal and growth factor responses to heavy resistance exercise protocols. *Journal of applied physiology (Bethesda, Md. : 1985), 69*(4), 1442-1450.

Liu, Y., Vertommen, D., Rider, M. H., & Lai, Y.-C. (2013). Mammalian target of rapamycin-independent S6K1 and 4E-BP1 phosphorylation during contraction in rat skeletal muscle. *Cellular signalling, 25*(9), 1877-1886.

Loenneke, J. P., Fahs, C. A., Rossow, L. M., Thiebaud, R. S., Mattocks, K. T., Abe, T., & Bemben, M. G. (2013). Blood flow restriction pressure recommendations: a tale of two cuffs. *Frontiers in physiology, 4*, 249.

Loenneke, J. P., Wilson, G. J., & Wilson, J. M. (2010). A

mechanistic approach to blood flow occlusion. *Int J Sports Med, 31*(1), 1-4. doi:10.1055/s-0029-1239499

MacDougall, J. D., Sale, D. G., Elder, G. C., & Sutton, J. R. (1982). Muscle ultrastructural characteristics of elite powerlifters and bodybuilders. *European journal of applied physiology and occupational physiology, 48*(1), 117-126.

Manini, T. M., & Clark, B. C. (2009). Blood flow restricted exercise and skeletal muscle health. *Exercise and sport sciences reviews, 37*(2), 78-85.

McCall, G. E., Byrnes, W. C., Dickinson, A., Pattany, P. M., & Fleck, S. J. (1996). Muscle fiber hypertrophy, hyperplasia, and capillary density in college men after resistance training. *Journal of applied physiology (Bethesda, Md. : 1985), 81*(5), 2004-2012.

Owens, J. (2016). *Blood Flow Restriction Rehabilitation*.

Patterson, S., Hughes, L., Warmington, S., Burr, J., Scott, B., Owens, J., . . . Loenneke, J. (2019). Blood Flow Restriction Exercise Position Stand: Considerations of Methodology, Application, and Safety. *Frontiers in Physiology, 10*, 533.

Pearson, S. J., & Hussain, S. R. (2015). A review on the mechanisms of blood-flow restriction resistance training-induced muscle hypertrophy. *Sports Med, 45*(2), 187-200. doi:10.1007/s40279-014-0264-9

Scott, B. R., Loenneke, J. P., Slattery, K. M., & Dascombe, B. J. (2015). Exercise with blood flow restriction: an updated evidence-based approach for enhanced muscular development. *Sports Med, 45*(3), 313-325. doi:10.1007/s40279-014-0288-1

Scott, B. R., Slattery, K. M., Sculley, D. V., & Dascombe, B. J.

(2014). Hypoxia and resistance exercise: a comparison of localized and systemic methods. *Sports Med, 44*(8), 1037-1054. doi:10.1007/s40279-014-0177-7

Vandenburgh, H., & Kaufman, S. (1979). In vitro model for stretch-induced hypertrophy of skeletal muscle. *Science (New York, N.Y.), 203*(4377), 265-268.

References

Dankel, S. J., Buckner, S. L., Jessee, M. B., Mattocks, K. T., Mouser, J. G., Counts, B. R., . . . Loenneke, J. P. (2018). Can blood flow restriction augment muscle activation during high-load training? *Clin Physiol Funct Imaging, 38*(2), 291-295. doi:10.1111/cpf.12414

Downs, M. E., Hackney, K. J., Martin, D., Caine, T. L., Cunningham, D., O'Connor, D. P., & Ploutz-Snyder, L. L. (2014). Acute vascular and cardiovascular responses to blood flow-restricted exercise. *Medicine and science in sports and exercise, 46*(8), 1489-1497.

Global, K. Retrieved from https://www.kaatsu-global.com/index.cfm?Action=About.Home#History

Goldberg, A. L., Etlinger, J. D., Goldspink, D. F., & Jablecki, C. (1975). Mechanism of work-induced hypertrophy of skeletal muscle. *Medicine and science in sports, 7*(3), 185-198.

Henneman, E., Somjen, G., & Carpenter, D. O. (1965). FUNCTIONAL SIGNIFICANCE OF CELL SIZE IN SPINAL

MOTONEURONS. *Journal of neurophysiology, 28*, 560-580.

Hylden, C., Burns, T., Stinner, D., & Owens, J. (2015). Blood flow restriction rehabilitation for extremity weakness: a case series. *J Spec Oper Med, 15*(1), 50-56.

Jessee, M. B., Mattocks, K. T., S.L., B., Dankel, S. J., Mouser, J. G., Abe, T., & Loenneke, J. P. (2018). Mechanisms of Blood Flow Restriction: The New Testament. *Techniques in Orthopaedics, Volume Publish Ahead of Print*.

Kraemer, W. J., Marchitelli, L., Gordon, S. E., Harman, E., Dziados, J. E., Mello, R., . . . Fleck, S. J. (1990). Hormonal and growth factor responses to heavy resistance exercise protocols. *Journal of applied physiology (Bethesda, Md. : 1985), 69*(4), 1442-1450.

Liu, Y., Vertommen, D., Rider, M. H., & Lai, Y.-C. (2013). Mammalian target of rapamycin-independent S6K1 and 4E-BP1 phosphorylation during contraction in rat skeletal muscle. *Cellular signalling, 25*(9), 1877-1886.

Loenneke, J. P., Fahs, C. A., Rossow, L. M., Thiebaud, R. S., Mattocks, K. T., Abe, T., & Bemben, M. G. (2013). Blood flow restriction pressure recommendations: a tale of two cuffs. *Frontiers in physiology, 4*, 249.

Loenneke, J. P., Wilson, G. J., & Wilson, J. M. (2010). A mechanistic approach to blood flow occlusion. *Int J Sports Med, 31*(1), 1-4. doi:10.1055/s-0029-1239499

MacDougall, J. D., Sale, D. G., Elder, G. C., & Sutton, J. R. (1982). Muscle ultrastructural characteristics of elite powerlifters and bodybuilders. *European journal of applied physiology and occupational physiology, 48*(1), 117-126.

Manini, T. M., & Clark, B. C. (2009). Blood flow restricted exercise and skeletal muscle health. *Exercise and sport sciences reviews, 37*(2), 78-85.

McCall, G. E., Byrnes, W. C., Dickinson, A., Pattany, P. M., & Fleck, S. J. (1996). Muscle fiber hypertrophy, hyperplasia, and capillary density in college men after resistance training. *Journal of applied physiology (Bethesda, Md. : 1985), 81*(5), 2004-2012.

Owens, J. (2016). *Blood Flow Restriction Rehabilitation*.

Patterson, S., Hughes, L., Warmington, S., Burr, J., Scott, B., Owens, J., . . . Loenneke, J. (2019). Blood Flow Restriction Exercise Position Stand: Considerations of Methodology, Application, and Safety. *Frontiers in Physiology, 10*, 533.

Pearson, S. J., & Hussain, S. R. (2015). A review on the mechanisms of blood-flow restriction resistance training-induced muscle hypertrophy. *Sports Med, 45*(2), 187-200. doi:10.1007/s40279-014-0264-9

Scott, B. R., Loenneke, J. P., Slattery, K. M., & Dascombe, B. J. (2015). Exercise with blood flow restriction: an updated evidence-based approach for enhanced muscular development. *Sports Med, 45*(3), 313-325. doi:10.1007/s40279-014-0288-1

Scott, B. R., Slattery, K. M., Sculley, D. V., & Dascombe, B. J. (2014). Hypoxia and resistance exercise: a comparison of localized and systemic methods. *Sports Med, 44*(8), 1037-1054. doi:10.1007/s40279-014-0177-7

Vandenburgh, H., & Kaufman, S. (1979). In vitro model for stretch-induced hypertrophy of skeletal muscle.

Science (New York, N.Y.), 203(4377), 265-268.

References

Dankel, S. J., Buckner, S. L., Jessee, M. B., Mattocks, K. T., Mouser, J. G., Counts, B. R., . . . Loenneke, J. P. (2018). Can blood flow restriction augment muscle activation during high-load training? *Clin Physiol Funct Imaging, 38*(2), 291-295. doi:10.1111/cpf.12414

Downs, M. E., Hackney, K. J., Martin, D., Caine, T. L., Cunningham, D., O'Connor, D. P., & Ploutz-Snyder, L. L. (2014). Acute vascular and cardiovascular responses to blood flow-restricted exercise. *Medicine and science in sports and exercise, 46*(8), 1489-1497.

Global, K. Retrieved from https://www.kaatsu-global.com/index.cfm?Action=About.Home#History

Goldberg, A. L., Etlinger, J. D., Goldspink, D. F., & Jablecki, C. (1975). Mechanism of work-induced hypertrophy of skeletal muscle. *Medicine and science in sports, 7*(3), 185-198.

Henneman, E., Somjen, G., & Carpenter, D. O. (1965). FUNCTIONAL SIGNIFICANCE OF CELL SIZE IN SPINAL MOTONEURONS. *Journal of neurophysiology, 28*, 560-580.

Hylden, C., Burns, T., Stinner, D., & Owens, J. (2015). Blood flow restriction rehabilitation for extremity weakness: a case series. *J Spec Oper Med, 15*(1), 50-56.

Jessee, M. B., Mattocks, K. T., S.L., B., Dankel, S. J., Mouser, J. G., Abe, T., & Loenneke, J. P. (2018). Mechanisms of Blood Flow Restriction: The New Testament. *Techniques in Orthopaedics, Volume Publish Ahead of Print.*

Kraemer, W. J., Marchitelli, L., Gordon, S. E., Harman, E., Dziados, J. E., Mello, R., . . . Fleck, S. J. (1990). Hormonal and growth factor responses to heavy resistance exercise protocols. *Journal of applied physiology (Bethesda, Md. : 1985), 69*(4), 1442-1450.

Liu, Y., Vertommen, D., Rider, M. H., & Lai, Y.-C. (2013). Mammalian target of rapamycin-independent S6K1 and 4E-BP1 phosphorylation during contraction in rat skeletal muscle. *Cellular signalling, 25*(9), 1877-1886.

Loenneke, J. P., Fahs, C. A., Rossow, L. M., Thiebaud, R. S., Mattocks, K. T., Abe, T., & Bemben, M. G. (2013). Blood flow restriction pressure recommendations: a tale of two cuffs. *Frontiers in physiology, 4*, 249.

Loenneke, J. P., Wilson, G. J., & Wilson, J. M. (2010). A mechanistic approach to blood flow occlusion. *Int J Sports Med, 31*(1), 1-4. doi:10.1055/s-0029-1239499

MacDougall, J. D., Sale, D. G., Elder, G. C., & Sutton, J. R. (1982). Muscle ultrastructural characteristics of elite powerlifters and bodybuilders. *European journal of applied physiology and occupational physiology, 48*(1), 117-126.

Manini, T. M., & Clark, B. C. (2009). Blood flow restricted exercise and skeletal muscle health. *Exercise and sport sciences reviews, 37*(2), 78-85.

McCall, G. E., Byrnes, W. C., Dickinson, A., Pattany, P. M., &

Fleck, S. J. (1996). Muscle fiber hypertrophy, hyperplasia, and capillary density in college men after resistance training. *Journal of applied physiology (Bethesda, Md. : 1985), 81*(5), 2004-2012.

Owens, J. (2016). *Blood Flow Restriction Rehabilitation*.

Patterson, S., Hughes, L., Warmington, S., Burr, J., Scott, B., Owens, J., . . . Loenneke, J. (2019). Blood Flow Restriction Exercise Position Stand: Considerations of Methodology, Application, and Safety. *Frontiers in Physiology, 10*, 533.

Pearson, S. J., & Hussain, S. R. (2015). A review on the mechanisms of blood-flow restriction resistance training-induced muscle hypertrophy. *Sports Med, 45*(2), 187-200. doi:10.1007/s40279-014-0264-9

Scott, B. R., Loenneke, J. P., Slattery, K. M., & Dascombe, B. J. (2015). Exercise with blood flow restriction: an updated evidence-based approach for enhanced muscular development. *Sports Med, 45*(3), 313-325. doi:10.1007/s40279-014-0288-1

Scott, B. R., Slattery, K. M., Sculley, D. V., & Dascombe, B. J. (2014). Hypoxia and resistance exercise: a comparison of localized and systemic methods. *Sports Med, 44*(8), 1037-1054. doi:10.1007/s40279-014-0177-7

Vandenburgh, H., & Kaufman, S. (1979). In vitro model for stretch-induced hypertrophy of skeletal muscle. *Science (New York, N.Y.), 203*(4377), 265-268.

References

Dankel, S. J., Buckner, S. L., Jessee, M. B., Mattocks, K. T., Mouser, J. G., Counts, B. R., . . . Loenneke, J. P. (2018). Can blood flow restriction augment muscle activation during high-load training? *Clin Physiol Funct Imaging, 38*(2), 291-295. doi:10.1111/cpf.12414

Downs, M. E., Hackney, K. J., Martin, D., Caine, T. L., Cunningham, D., O'Connor, D. P., & Ploutz-Snyder, L. L. (2014). Acute vascular and cardiovascular responses to blood flow-restricted exercise. *Medicine and science in sports and exercise, 46*(8), 1489-1497.

Global, K. Retrieved from https://www.kaatsu-global.com/index.cfm?Action=About.Home#History

Goldberg, A. L., Etlinger, J. D., Goldspink, D. F., & Jablecki, C. (1975). Mechanism of work-induced hypertrophy of skeletal muscle. *Medicine and science in sports, 7*(3), 185-198.

Henneman, E., Somjen, G., & Carpenter, D. O. (1965). FUNCTIONAL SIGNIFICANCE OF CELL SIZE IN SPINAL MOTONEURONS. *Journal of neurophysiology, 28*, 560-580.

Hylden, C., Burns, T., Stinner, D., & Owens, J. (2015). Blood flow restriction rehabilitation for extremity weakness: a case series. *J Spec Oper Med, 15*(1), 50-56.

Jessee, M. B., Mattocks, K. T., S.L., B., Dankel, S. J., Mouser, J. G., Abe, T., & Loenneke, J. P. (2018). Mechanisms of Blood Flow Restriction: The New Testament. *Techniques in Orthopaedics, Volume Publish Ahead of Print*.

Kraemer, W. J., Marchitelli, L., Gordon, S. E., Harman, E.,

Dziados, J. E., Mello, R., . . . Fleck, S. J. (1990). Hormonal and growth factor responses to heavy resistance exercise protocols. *Journal of applied physiology (Bethesda, Md. : 1985), 69*(4), 1442-1450.

Liu, Y., Vertommen, D., Rider, M. H., & Lai, Y.-C. (2013). Mammalian target of rapamycin-independent S6K1 and 4E-BP1 phosphorylation during contraction in rat skeletal muscle. *Cellular signalling, 25*(9), 1877-1886.

Loenneke, J. P., Fahs, C. A., Rossow, L. M., Thiebaud, R. S., Mattocks, K. T., Abe, T., & Bemben, M. G. (2013). Blood flow restriction pressure recommendations: a tale of two cuffs. *Frontiers in physiology, 4*, 249.

Loenneke, J. P., Wilson, G. J., & Wilson, J. M. (2010). A mechanistic approach to blood flow occlusion. *Int J Sports Med, 31*(1), 1-4. doi:10.1055/s-0029-1239499

MacDougall, J. D., Sale, D. G., Elder, G. C., & Sutton, J. R. (1982). Muscle ultrastructural characteristics of elite powerlifters and bodybuilders. *European journal of applied physiology and occupational physiology, 48*(1), 117-126.

Manini, T. M., & Clark, B. C. (2009). Blood flow restricted exercise and skeletal muscle health. *Exercise and sport sciences reviews, 37*(2), 78-85.

McCall, G. E., Byrnes, W. C., Dickinson, A., Pattany, P. M., & Fleck, S. J. (1996). Muscle fiber hypertrophy, hyperplasia, and capillary density in college men after resistance training. *Journal of applied physiology (Bethesda, Md. : 1985), 81*(5), 2004-2012.

Owens, J. (2016). *Blood Flow Restriction Rehabilitation.*

Patterson, S., Hughes, L., Warmington, S., Burr, J., Scott, B., Owens, J., . . . Loenneke, J. (2019). Blood Flow Restriction Exercise Position Stand: Considerations of Methodology, Application, and Safety. *Frontiers in Physiology, 10*, 533.

Pearson, S. J., & Hussain, S. R. (2015). A review on the mechanisms of blood-flow restriction resistance training-induced muscle hypertrophy. *Sports Med, 45*(2), 187-200. doi:10.1007/s40279-014-0264-9

Scott, B. R., Loenneke, J. P., Slattery, K. M., & Dascombe, B. J. (2015). Exercise with blood flow restriction: an updated evidence-based approach for enhanced muscular development. *Sports Med, 45*(3), 313-325. doi:10.1007/s40279-014-0288-1

Scott, B. R., Slattery, K. M., Sculley, D. V., & Dascombe, B. J. (2014). Hypoxia and resistance exercise: a comparison of localized and systemic methods. *Sports Med, 44*(8), 1037-1054. doi:10.1007/s40279-014-0177-7

Vandenburgh, H., & Kaufman, S. (1979). In vitro model for stretch-induced hypertrophy of skeletal muscle. *Science (New York, N.Y.), 203*(4377), 265-268.

References

Dankel, S. J., Buckner, S. L., Jessee, M. B., Mattocks, K. T., Mouser, J. G., Counts, B. R., . . . Loenneke, J. P. (2018). Can blood flow restriction augment muscle activation during high-load training? *Clin Physiol Funct Imaging, 38*(2), 291-295. doi:10.1111/cpf.12414

Downs, M. E., Hackney, K. J., Martin, D., Caine, T. L., Cunningham, D., O'Connor, D. P., & Ploutz-Snyder, L. L. (2014). Acute vascular and cardiovascular responses to blood flow-restricted exercise. *Medicine and science in sports and exercise, 46*(8), 1489-1497.

Global, K. Retrieved from https://www.kaatsu-global.com/index.cfm?Action=About.Home#History

Goldberg, A. L., Etlinger, J. D., Goldspink, D. F., & Jablecki, C. (1975). Mechanism of work-induced hypertrophy of skeletal muscle. *Medicine and science in sports, 7*(3), 185-198.

Henneman, E., Somjen, G., & Carpenter, D. O. (1965). FUNCTIONAL SIGNIFICANCE OF CELL SIZE IN SPINAL MOTONEURONS. *Journal of neurophysiology, 28*, 560-580.

Hylden, C., Burns, T., Stinner, D., & Owens, J. (2015). Blood flow restriction rehabilitation for extremity weakness: a case series. *J Spec Oper Med, 15*(1), 50-56.

Jessee, M. B., Mattocks, K. T., S.L., B., Dankel, S. J., Mouser, J. G., Abe, T., & Loenneke, J. P. (2018). Mechanisms of Blood Flow Restriction: The New Testament. *Techniques in Orthopaedics, Volume Publish Ahead of Print*.

Kraemer, W. J., Marchitelli, L., Gordon, S. E., Harman, E., Dziados, J. E., Mello, R., . . . Fleck, S. J. (1990). Hormonal and growth factor responses to heavy resistance exercise protocols. *Journal of applied physiology (Bethesda, Md. : 1985), 69*(4), 1442-1450.

Liu, Y., Vertommen, D., Rider, M. H., & Lai, Y.-C. (2013).

Mammalian target of rapamycin-independent S6K1 and 4E-BP1 phosphorylation during contraction in rat skeletal muscle. *Cellular signalling, 25*(9), 1877-1886.

Loenneke, J. P., Fahs, C. A., Rossow, L. M., Thiebaud, R. S., Mattocks, K. T., Abe, T., & Bemben, M. G. (2013). Blood flow restriction pressure recommendations: a tale of two cuffs. *Frontiers in physiology, 4*, 249.

Loenneke, J. P., Wilson, G. J., & Wilson, J. M. (2010). A mechanistic approach to blood flow occlusion. *Int J Sports Med, 31*(1), 1-4. doi:10.1055/s-0029-1239499

MacDougall, J. D., Sale, D. G., Elder, G. C., & Sutton, J. R. (1982). Muscle ultrastructural characteristics of elite powerlifters and bodybuilders. *European journal of applied physiology and occupational physiology, 48*(1), 117-126.

Manini, T. M., & Clark, B. C. (2009). Blood flow restricted exercise and skeletal muscle health. *Exercise and sport sciences reviews, 37*(2), 78-85.

McCall, G. E., Byrnes, W. C., Dickinson, A., Pattany, P. M., & Fleck, S. J. (1996). Muscle fiber hypertrophy, hyperplasia, and capillary density in college men after resistance training. *Journal of applied physiology (Bethesda, Md. : 1985), 81*(5), 2004-2012.

Owens, J. (2016). *Blood Flow Restriction Rehabilitation*.

Patterson, S., Hughes, L., Warmington, S., Burr, J., Scott, B., Owens, J., . . . Loenneke, J. (2019). Blood Flow Restriction Exercise Position Stand: Considerations of Methodology, Application, and Safety. *Frontiers in Physiology, 10*, 533.

Pearson, S. J., & Hussain, S. R. (2015). A review on the

mechanisms of blood-flow restriction resistance training-induced muscle hypertrophy. *Sports Med, 45*(2), 187-200. doi:10.1007/s40279-014-0264-9

Scott, B. R., Loenneke, J. P., Slattery, K. M., & Dascombe, B. J. (2015). Exercise with blood flow restriction: an updated evidence-based approach for enhanced muscular development. *Sports Med, 45*(3), 313-325. doi:10.1007/s40279-014-0288-1

Scott, B. R., Slattery, K. M., Sculley, D. V., & Dascombe, B. J. (2014). Hypoxia and resistance exercise: a comparison of localized and systemic methods. *Sports Med, 44*(8), 1037-1054. doi:10.1007/s40279-014-0177-7

Vandenburgh, H., & Kaufman, S. (1979). In vitro model for stretch-induced hypertrophy of skeletal muscle. *Science (New York, N.Y.), 203*(4377), 265-268.

References

Dankel, S. J., Buckner, S. L., Jessee, M. B., Mattocks, K. T., Mouser, J. G., Counts, B. R., . . . Loenneke, J. P. (2018). Can blood flow restriction augment muscle activation during high-load training? *Clin Physiol Funct Imaging, 38*(2), 291-295. doi:10.1111/cpf.12414

Downs, M. E., Hackney, K. J., Martin, D., Caine, T. L., Cunningham, D., O'Connor, D. P., & Ploutz-Snyder, L. L. (2014). Acute vascular and cardiovascular responses to blood flow-restricted exercise. *Medicine and science in sports and exercise, 46*(8), 1489-1497.

Global, K. Retrieved from https://www.kaatsu-global.com/index.cfm?Action=About.Home#History

Goldberg, A. L., Etlinger, J. D., Goldspink, D. F., & Jablecki, C. (1975). Mechanism of work-induced hypertrophy of skeletal muscle. *Medicine and science in sports, 7*(3), 185-198.

Henneman, E., Somjen, G., & Carpenter, D. O. (1965). FUNCTIONAL SIGNIFICANCE OF CELL SIZE IN SPINAL MOTONEURONS. *Journal of neurophysiology, 28*, 560-580.

Hylden, C., Burns, T., Stinner, D., & Owens, J. (2015). Blood flow restriction rehabilitation for extremity weakness: a case series. *J Spec Oper Med, 15*(1), 50-56.

Jessee, M. B., Mattocks, K. T., S.L., B., Dankel, S. J., Mouser, J. G., Abe, T., & Loenneke, J. P. (2018). Mechanisms of Blood Flow Restriction: The New Testament. *Techniques in Orthopaedics, Volume Publish Ahead of Print.*

Kraemer, W. J., Marchitelli, L., Gordon, S. E., Harman, E., Dziados, J. E., Mello, R., . . . Fleck, S. J. (1990). Hormonal and growth factor responses to heavy resistance exercise protocols. *Journal of applied physiology (Bethesda, Md. : 1985), 69*(4), 1442-1450.

Liu, Y., Vertommen, D., Rider, M. H., & Lai, Y.-C. (2013). Mammalian target of rapamycin-independent S6K1 and 4E-BP1 phosphorylation during contraction in rat skeletal muscle. *Cellular signalling, 25*(9), 1877-1886.

Loenneke, J. P., Fahs, C. A., Rossow, L. M., Thiebaud, R. S., Mattocks, K. T., Abe, T., & Bemben, M. G. (2013).

Blood flow restriction pressure recommendations: a tale of two cuffs. *Frontiers in physiology, 4*, 249.

Loenneke, J. P., Wilson, G. J., & Wilson, J. M. (2010). A mechanistic approach to blood flow occlusion. *Int J Sports Med, 31*(1), 1-4. doi:10.1055/s-0029-1239499

MacDougall, J. D., Sale, D. G., Elder, G. C., & Sutton, J. R. (1982). Muscle ultrastructural characteristics of elite powerlifters and bodybuilders. *European journal of applied physiology and occupational physiology, 48*(1), 117-126.

Manini, T. M., & Clark, B. C. (2009). Blood flow restricted exercise and skeletal muscle health. *Exercise and sport sciences reviews, 37*(2), 78-85.

McCall, G. E., Byrnes, W. C., Dickinson, A., Pattany, P. M., & Fleck, S. J. (1996). Muscle fiber hypertrophy, hyperplasia, and capillary density in college men after resistance training. *Journal of applied physiology (Bethesda, Md. : 1985), 81*(5), 2004-2012.

Owens, J. (2016). *Blood Flow Restriction Rehabilitation*.

Patterson, S., Hughes, L., Warmington, S., Burr, J., Scott, B., Owens, J., . . . Loenneke, J. (2019). Blood Flow Restriction Exercise Position Stand: Considerations of Methodology, Application, and Safety. *Frontiers in Physiology, 10*, 533.

Pearson, S. J., & Hussain, S. R. (2015). A review on the mechanisms of blood-flow restriction resistance training-induced muscle hypertrophy. *Sports Med, 45*(2), 187-200. doi:10.1007/s40279-014-0264-9

Scott, B. R., Loenneke, J. P., Slattery, K. M., & Dascombe, B. J. (2015). Exercise with blood flow restriction: an updated evidence-based approach for enhanced muscular development. *Sports Med, 45*(3), 313-325. doi:10.1007/s40279-014-0288-1

Scott, B. R., Slattery, K. M., Sculley, D. V., & Dascombe, B. J. (2014). Hypoxia and resistance exercise: a comparison of localized and systemic methods. *Sports Med, 44*(8), 1037-1054. doi:10.1007/s40279-014-0177-7

Vandenburgh, H., & Kaufman, S. (1979). In vitro model for stretch-induced hypertrophy of skeletal muscle. *Science (New York, N.Y.), 203*(4377), 265-268.

References

Dankel, S. J., Buckner, S. L., Jessee, M. B., Mattocks, K. T., Mouser, J. G., Counts, B. R., . . . Loenneke, J. P. (2018). Can blood flow restriction augment muscle activation during high-load training? *Clin Physiol Funct Imaging, 38*(2), 291-295. doi:10.1111/cpf.12414

Downs, M. E., Hackney, K. J., Martin, D., Caine, T. L., Cunningham, D., O'Connor, D. P., & Ploutz-Snyder, L. L. (2014). Acute vascular and cardiovascular responses to blood flow-restricted exercise. *Medicine and science in sports and exercise, 46*(8), 1489-1497.

Global, K. Retrieved from https://www.kaatsu-global.com/index.cfm?Action=About.Home#History

Goldberg, A. L., Etlinger, J. D., Goldspink, D. F., & Jablecki, C. (1975). Mechanism of work-induced hypertrophy of skeletal muscle. *Medicine and* science in sports, 7(3), 185-198.

Henneman, E., Somjen, G., & Carpenter, D. O. (1965). FUNCTIONAL SIGNIFICANCE OF CELL SIZE IN SPINAL MOTONEURONS. *Journal of neurophysiology, 28,* 560-580.

Hylden, C., Burns, T., Stinner, D., & Owens, J. (2015). Blood flow restriction rehabilitation for extremity weakness: a case series. *J Spec Oper Med, 15*(1), 50-56.

Jessee, M. B., Mattocks, K. T., S.L., B., Dankel, S. J., Mouser, J. G., Abe, T., & Loenneke, J. P. (2018). Mechanisms of Blood Flow Restriction: The New Testament. *Techniques in Orthopaedics, Volume Publish Ahead of Print.*

Kraemer, W. J., Marchitelli, L., Gordon, S. E., Harman, E., Dziados, J. E., Mello, R., . . . Fleck, S. J. (1990). Hormonal and growth factor responses to heavy resistance exercise protocols. *Journal of applied physiology (Bethesda, Md. : 1985), 69*(4), 1442-1450.

Liu, Y., Vertommen, D., Rider, M. H., & Lai, Y.-C. (2013). Mammalian target of rapamycin-independent S6K1 and 4E-BP1 phosphorylation during contraction in rat skeletal muscle. *Cellular signalling, 25*(9), 1877-1886.

Loenneke, J. P., Fahs, C. A., Rossow, L. M., Thiebaud, R. S., Mattocks, K. T., Abe, T., & Bemben, M. G. (2013). Blood flow restriction pressure recommendations: a tale of two cuffs. *Frontiers in physiology, 4,* 249.

Loenneke, J. P., Wilson, G. J., & Wilson, J. M. (2010). A mechanistic approach to blood flow occlusion. *Int J Sports Med, 31*(1), 1-4. doi:10.1055/s-0029-1239499

MacDougall, J. D., Sale, D. G., Elder, G. C., & Sutton, J. R. (1982). Muscle ultrastructural characteristics of elite powerlifters and bodybuilders. *European journal of applied physiology and occupational physiology, 48*(1), 117-126.

Manini, T. M., & Clark, B. C. (2009). Blood flow restricted exercise and skeletal muscle health. *Exercise and sport sciences reviews, 37*(2), 78-85.

McCall, G. E., Byrnes, W. C., Dickinson, A., Pattany, P. M., & Fleck, S. J. (1996). Muscle fiber hypertrophy, hyperplasia, and capillary density in college men after resistance training. *Journal of applied physiology (Bethesda, Md. : 1985), 81*(5), 2004-2012.

Owens, J. (2016). *Blood Flow Restriction Rehabilitation*.

Patterson, S., Hughes, L., Warmington, S., Burr, J., Scott, B., Owens, J., . . . Loenneke, J. (2019). Blood Flow Restriction Exercise Position Stand: Considerations of Methodology, Application, and Safety. *Frontiers in Physiology, 10*, 533.

Pearson, S. J., & Hussain, S. R. (2015). A review on the mechanisms of blood-flow restriction resistance training-induced muscle hypertrophy. *Sports Med, 45*(2), 187-200. doi:10.1007/s40279-014-0264-9

Scott, B. R., Loenneke, J. P., Slattery, K. M., & Dascombe, B. J. (2015). Exercise with blood flow restriction: an updated evidence-based approach for enhanced muscular development. *Sports Med, 45*(3), 313-325. doi:10.1007/s40279-014-0288-1

Scott, B. R., Slattery, K. M., Sculley, D. V., & Dascombe, B. J. (2014). Hypoxia and resistance exercise: a comparison of localized and systemic methods. *Sports Med, 44*(8), 1037-1054. doi:10.1007/s40279-

014-0177-7

Vandenburgh, H., & Kaufman, S. (1979). In vitro model for stretch-induced hypertrophy of skeletal muscle. *Science (New York, N.Y.), 203*(4377), 265-268.

References

Dankel, S. J., Buckner, S. L., Jessee, M. B., Mattocks, K. T., Mouser, J. G., Counts, B. R., . . . Loenneke, J. P. (2018). Can blood flow restriction augment muscle activation during high-load training? *Clin Physiol Funct Imaging, 38*(2), 291-295. doi:10.1111/cpf.12414

Downs, M. E., Hackney, K. J., Martin, D., Caine, T. L., Cunningham, D., O'Connor, D. P., & Ploutz-Snyder, L. L. (2014). Acute vascular and cardiovascular responses to blood flow-restricted exercise. *Medicine and science in sports and exercise, 46*(8), 1489-1497.

Global, K. Retrieved from https://www.kaatsu-global.com/index.cfm?Action=About.Home#History

Goldberg, A. L., Etlinger, J. D., Goldspink, D. F., & Jablecki, C. (1975). Mechanism of work-induced hypertrophy of skeletal muscle. *Medicine and science in sports, 7*(3), 185-198.

Henneman, E., Somjen, G., & Carpenter, D. O. (1965). FUNCTIONAL SIGNIFICANCE OF CELL SIZE IN SPINAL MOTONEURONS. *Journal of neurophysiology, 28*, 560-580.

Hylden, C., Burns, T., Stinner, D., & Owens, J. (2015). Blood flow restriction rehabilitation for extremity weakness: a case series. *J Spec Oper Med, 15*(1), 50-56.

Jessee, M. B., Mattocks, K. T., S.L., B., Dankel, S. J., Mouser, J. G., Abe, T., & Loenneke, J. P. (2018). Mechanisms of Blood Flow Restriction: The New Testament. *Techniques in Orthopaedics, Volume Publish Ahead of Print.*

Kraemer, W. J., Marchitelli, L., Gordon, S. E., Harman, E., Dziados, J. E., Mello, R., . . . Fleck, S. J. (1990). Hormonal and growth factor responses to heavy resistance exercise protocols. *Journal of applied physiology (Bethesda, Md. : 1985), 69*(4), 1442-1450.

Liu, Y., Vertommen, D., Rider, M. H., & Lai, Y.-C. (2013). Mammalian target of rapamycin-independent S6K1 and 4E-BP1 phosphorylation during contraction in rat skeletal muscle. *Cellular signalling, 25*(9), 1877-1886.

Loenneke, J. P., Fahs, C. A., Rossow, L. M., Thiebaud, R. S., Mattocks, K. T., Abe, T., & Bemben, M. G. (2013). Blood flow restriction pressure recommendations: a tale of two cuffs. *Frontiers in physiology, 4*, 249.

Loenneke, J. P., Wilson, G. J., & Wilson, J. M. (2010). A mechanistic approach to blood flow occlusion. *Int J Sports Med, 31*(1), 1-4. doi:10.1055/s-0029-1239499

MacDougall, J. D., Sale, D. G., Elder, G. C., & Sutton, J. R. (1982). Muscle ultrastructural characteristics of elite powerlifters and bodybuilders. *European journal of applied physiology and occupational physiology, 48*(1), 117-126.

Manini, T. M., & Clark, B. C. (2009). Blood flow restricted

exercise and skeletal muscle health. *Exercise and sport sciences reviews, 37*(2), 78-85.

McCall, G. E., Byrnes, W. C., Dickinson, A., Pattany, P. M., & Fleck, S. J. (1996). Muscle fiber hypertrophy, hyperplasia, and capillary density in college men after resistance training. *Journal of applied physiology (Bethesda, Md. : 1985), 81*(5), 2004-2012.

Owens, J. (2016). *Blood Flow Restriction Rehabilitation*.

Patterson, S., Hughes, L., Warmington, S., Burr, J., Scott, B., Owens, J., . . . Loenneke, J. (2019). Blood Flow Restriction Exercise Position Stand: Considerations of Methodology, Application, and Safety. *Frontiers in Physiology, 10*, 533.

Pearson, S. J., & Hussain, S. R. (2015). A review on the mechanisms of blood-flow restriction resistance training-induced muscle hypertrophy. *Sports Med, 45*(2), 187-200. doi:10.1007/s40279-014-0264-9

Scott, B. R., Loenneke, J. P., Slattery, K. M., & Dascombe, B. J. (2015). Exercise with blood flow restriction: an updated evidence-based approach for enhanced muscular development. *Sports Med, 45*(3), 313-325. doi:10.1007/s40279-014-0288-1

Scott, B. R., Slattery, K. M., Sculley, D. V., & Dascombe, B. J. (2014). Hypoxia and resistance exercise: a comparison of localized and systemic methods. *Sports Med, 44*(8), 1037-1054. doi:10.1007/s40279-014-0177-7

Vandenburgh, H., & Kaufman, S. (1979). In vitro model for stretch-induced hypertrophy of skeletal muscle. *Science (New York, N.Y.), 203*(4377), 265-268.

Printed in Great Britain
by Amazon